What Your Colleagues Are Saying . . .

"This timely book explores essential leadership topics with practical guidance and reflective insights. A must-read for education leaders, it promotes collaboration, emotional well-being, and growth. From refining coaching systems to embracing feedback, it equips leaders to adapt, thrive, and foster thriving communities—offering a transformative journey toward resilience and sustainable leadership excellence."

—Jennifer Benson
Assistant Principal, Rochester Public Schools
Rochester, Minnesota

"This book is like hiring your own personal leadership coach. The authors understand that real learning follows a metacognitive cycle of self-reflection, goal-setting, and new learning, and it means that the very practical lessons for leadership from this book won't be read and forgotten—they will lead to powerful changes in your leadership practices."

—Mark Hillman
Director of Teaching and Learning,
Georgetown International Academy
Georgetown, Guyana

"This book is a must-read for every school leader looking to nurture their resiliency skills, while empowering educators to do the same. Discover practical strategies to lead with self-care, grace, and resilience, even in the most challenging times! This book will help you be the leader every educator needs."

—Jessica Johnson
District Administrator, Dodgeland School District
Juneau, Wisconsin

"*Habits of Resilient School Leaders* offers educators a roadmap to self-care and personal sustainability. Packed with practical strategies for daily, weekly, and yearly leadership challenges, this book compassionately reminds leaders that prioritizing themselves isn't selfish—it is essential. A must-read for educators seeking sustainable success, it's like having a supportive coach in your corner."

—Jessica Lee Lovell
Principal, Sierra Vista High School
Las Vegas, Nevada

"This is one of the best books I have had the privilege to read in some time. It offers suggestions for how to thrive as a leader within one of the most challenging eras in education. It is chock-full of strategies and suggestions that can be immediately implemented and measured for impact."

—Lynn Lisy-Macan
Retired Superintendent
Bluffton, South Carolina

"This book provides a road map for leaders by defining resilience as actively leveraging difficult experiences for personal and organizational growth. It provides the right habits; leaders can create a positive and empowering environment that benefits everyone involved. This is a resourceful tool that won't sit on a shelf."

—Debra Paradowski
Associate Principal, Mukwonago High School
Waukesha, Wisconsin

"This book is ideal for school administrators and aspiring leaders seeking practical tools to balance personal well-being with professional impact. It is a comprehensive, empowering resource that inspires growth, resilience, and lasting change in schools. Ten thoughtfully crafted chapters provide simple strategies for school leaders to balance priorities, overcome challenges, and elevate their impact on school communities."

—Katie Ann Schafer
Principal, Pine Island Middle School
Pine Island, Minnesota

"As a veteran administrator, this book helped me reflect on where I have been as a leader (strengths and weaknesses), where I am now, and what I can do to be better moving forward. It left me energized and reminded me of my *why* for being an educational leader."

—Leslie Standerfer
Assistant Superintendent of Academics,
Buckeye Union School District
Litchfield Park, Arizona

Habits of Resilient School Leaders

Habits of Resilient School Leaders

Personal Practices That Drive Professional Impact

Lindsay Prendergast
Piper Lee

Foreword by Dominique Smith

A Joint Publication

CORWIN

FOR INFORMATION:

Corwin

A SAGE Company

2455 Teller Road

Thousand Oaks, California 91320

(800) 233-9936

www.corwin.com

SAGE Publications Ltd.

1 Oliver's Yard

55 City Road

London EC1Y 1SP

United Kingdom

SAGE Publications India Pvt. Ltd.

Unit No 323-333, Third Floor, F-Block

International Trade Tower Nehru Place

New Delhi 110 019

India

SAGE Publications Asia-Pacific Pte. Ltd.

18 Cross Street #10-10/11/12

China Square Central

Singapore 048423

Paperback ISBN 978-1-0719-6286-2

Vice President and
   Editorial Director: Monica Eckman

Senior Acquisitions Editor: Pam Berkman

Content Development
   Manager: Desirée A. Bartlett

Development Editor: Sara Johnson

Senior Editorial Assistant: Nyle De Leon

Production Editor: Tori Mirsadjadi

Copy Editor: Beth Ginter

Typesetter: C&M Digitals (P) Ltd.

Cover Designer: Candice Harman

Marketing Manager: Melissa Duclos

Contents

Visit the *Habits of Resilient Leaders* companion website at
https://companion.corwin.com/courses/resilientleaders
for downloadable resources.

Foreword

Early in my career as an aspiring leader, I saw Principal Baruti K. Kafele speak. He asked the audience a simple question: "Is your school better because you lead it?" That question sparked a drive in me to make sure I was doing everything in my power to make sure the school I led was better for our students, colleagues, families, and community. That question still guides my daily work in our school and the way that I plan for the future of our organization.

Now, over ten years later, I still have that spark. I work every day to ensure that I live up to those expectations, which requires that I address the new issues that arise daily. Unfortunately, I have seen some of my colleagues struggle during their first years of leadership. They experience the frustration that comes with leading adults and burnout generated by long days and family expectations. Although these emotions can come to the front of every educator's mind, the one area we can continue to focus on, and which is this book's backbone, is leaders' resilience. As leaders we can make the changes needed, and support our teachers and students, if we are resilient during the hard times and celebrate the times of success.

Leadership should be a praised position in our field, and we need to reclaim that feeling. *Habits of Resilient School Leaders: Personal Practices That Drive Professional Impact* by Lindsay Prendergast and Piper Lee helps leaders reexamine their own resilience by producing practical habits that leaders can use to have a successful career. The real-life examples and vignettes put you directly into a reflection mode to help you as a leader explore your own values, beliefs, and ideas. As a leader, I appreciate the return to habits and the focus on the small areas that can slip our minds as we go through the everyday life as a leader. The authors push you to think of how you set your own boundaries and create a meaningful space for feedback, protecting your own personal well-being while navigating your school toward a true vision. With years of experience in leadership, these authors have created a book that is resourceful for any leader no matter the experience. This book is not built for just administrators but anyone who is exploring or currently in a leadership role. I appreciated that practical habits can hold myself and the team I lead in a space to have success. After reading this book, I have seen myself refocus on being a lead learner, checking my blind spots and making sure I balance my work-life experience. As I was questioned in the beginning of my career, "Is your school better because you lead it?" I believe by working on these habits I could say, "Yes." I encourage every leader to take the time to dive deeper into this book because this is not just a book, but a guide to your journey as an educator. This work will never be the easiest, but by having a road map like this book to guide our practices, I hope to see more and more leaders not wanting to leave this profession or leave their schools but rather thrive as resilient school leaders.

—Dominique Smith

Acknowledgments

First and foremost, we extend our heartfelt appreciation to the endless encouragement of Piper and Lindsay's parents, Piper's children, and Lindsay's husband Pete, whose unwavering encouragement and sacrifices have played an integral role in bringing this book from just another dream all the way to publication. Our families have been a constant wellspring of support and understanding, providing the encouragement and patience necessary for us to dedicate ourselves to the research and writing of this book.

This book also stands as a testament to the remarkable individuals who have graciously shared their stories, insights, and experiences with us. Their willingness to engage and collaborate has been instrumental in the creation of the valuable lessons and knowledge presented within these pages. We are deeply grateful for the support and leadership of our colleagues at Corwin who have provided unwavering moral and professional encouragement and enabled us to bring this project to fruition. Special thanks to our fellow Corwin authors, Dr. Jeffrey Wilhelm, Dr. Thomas Guskey, and our incredible thought partners including Lindsay Deacon, Lori Stollar, and many others for their invaluable expertise and support throughout the journey.

PUBLISHER'S ACKNOWLEDGMENTS

Corwin gratefully acknowledges the contributions of the following reviewers:

Jessica Johnson
District Administrator, Dodgeland School District
Juneau, Wisconsin

Lynn Lisy-Macan
Retired Superintendent
Bluffton, South Carolina

Debra Paradowski
Associate Principal, Mukwonago High School
Waukesha, Wisconsin

Lena Marie Rockwood
Assistant Principal, Revere High School
Revere, Massachusetts

Leslie Standerfer
Assistant Superintendent of Academics,
Buckeye Union School District
Litchfield Park, Arizona

About the Authors

Lindsay Prendergast brings nearly two decades of experience in global education, where her roles have ranged from leadership coach to principal, consultant, and classroom teacher. As the assistant director of strategy and development with the Danielson Group, she collaborates with districts, schools, and educators to promote equitable teaching and learning through the Framework for Teaching. Lindsay's work centers on leading systems change and advancing instructional leadership with practical and impactful insights. Recognized as an ASCD Emerging Leader and Champion in Education as well as an AAIE Fellow, Lindsay is an established thought leader who frequently shares her expertise on leadership development, growth-centered supervision, and assessment practices through ASCD, Learning Forward, Edutopia, AAIE, EARCOS, AMLE, Cognia, and more. She coauthored best-selling *Habits of Resilient Educators: Strategies for Thriving During Times of Anxiety, Doubt, and Constant Change* (Prendergast & Lee, 2024), as well as dozens of articles and manuscripts in the field of education. Driven by a commitment to impactful change and global competence, Lindsay's work empowers educators to navigate complex challenges, fostering environments where both teachers and students thrive. Lindsay holds a bachelor's degree from Wofford College, a master's degree in education leadership from Colorado Western State University, and a doctoral degree in education leadership from Wilkes University.

Piper Lee has more than twenty-five years of experience in education, including teaching, administration, instructional coaching, professional learning facilitation, and leadership coaching. Her passion for student and adult learning and improving effective teacher instruction and student success in learning ignited her pursuit of working as an instructional leadership coach nationally. Over the course of her career, Piper has served students, families, teachers, leadership teams, and undergraduate and graduate students. Most recently, Piper has been supporting district leaders, principals, and educators in one of the largest school districts in the country. While partnering with educators across the country, Piper has learned and lives the philosophy that rigorous relationships help create transformative schools and impact every aspect of our lives. Piper received her bachelor of arts degree in elementary education, her master's degree in curriculum and instruction, and her education leadership certification and licensure from Winona State University in Minnesota.

Introduction

WHY THIS BOOK? WHY YOU?

Leadership, like teaching, can and should be a joyful profession where practitioners feel a sense of pride and accomplishment in their work. Yet worldwide, there is a sense of hopelessness around changing the contemporary culture of chaos. Studies show that the attrition rate of education leaders in K–12 schools worldwide has been steadily increasing at an alarming rate (NASSP & LPI, 2022), and systems may struggle to fill leadership roles for years to come. While similar to the data seen around classroom educators exiting the profession, this issue is receiving far less media attention. Therefore, we must shift the narrative. As authors, we are a team of eternal optimists with deep experience and endless admiration for education leaders. We aim to empower education leaders with a framework that enables them to regain control of their mindset and their practice despite their daily encounters with factors outside their control. The habits of personal and professional practice described in this book focus on adult well-being as seen through the lens of effective learning environments in schools and districts. In support of every leader's right to experience sustained confidence, fulfillment, and joy in their career, you will find that the chapters of this book provide authentic, proven practices that extend beyond self-care or managerial skills and provide a framework for you to sustain your journey without impacting your health. Let us dive in!

THE IMPERATIVE TO ADDRESS LEADER WELL-BEING: RESILIENCE IS KEY

Education leaders today need simple, proven habits that will equip them for the contemporary educational landscape. Administrators' well-being matters to themselves and the teachers, communities, and students they serve. School leaders are expected to support students, teachers, and the broader school community. This emotional labor, including managing crises, conflicts, and the well-being of staff and students, often takes a toll on their own mental health. Stress and burnout are closely associated with high turnover rates among school leaders, which disrupts school continuity and affects student learning outcomes. Resilience, however, is an effective mindset comprised of many factors that may be intentionally developed and serve to mitigate the effects of stress, burnout, and environments characterized by constant uncertainty.

The American Psychological Association defines resilience as "the process and outcome of successfully adapting to difficult or challenging life experiences, especially through mental, emotional, and behavioral flexibility and adjustment to external and internal demands" (American Psychological Association, n.d.). These processes are critical for leaders striving to sustain well-being amidst their myriad complexities and challenges. Education environments are constantly evolving due to curriculum changes, policy shifts, technological advancements, or unexpected events (like pandemics). Leaders who have developed resilience can better adapt to these changes while maintaining stability for their staff and students. A resilient leader models perseverance, optimism, and emotional intelligence, which can foster a school culture that encourages these same traits in teachers and students. By understanding resilience through the habits related to leading an education system within these chapters, leaders can invest in their well-being and that of their entire community.

A resilient leader models perseverance, optimism, and emotional intelligence, which can foster a school culture that encourages these same traits in teachers and students.

The habits described in this book each play a unique role in contributing toward your ability to develop and experience resilience. For example, a distinct aspect of resilient individuals is the experience of efficacy or belief in their ability to do their work well (Goddard et al., 2004). This construct links to the broader observation of sociocultural theory that we all have a vast network of influences that encourage or discourage us from believing in our ability to affect change. The habits of resilient leaders described herein are all focused on creating a positive and supportive network of influences that can enable those beliefs for individual leaders and support them in creating that social context for those they serve. In this way, we hope to show that these habits aren't *life hacks* capable of solving any problem but small practices that collectively create a context within which leaders can grow and develop as influential instructional leaders while navigating the complexities of contemporary education.

HOW DO HABITS INFLUENCE YOUR RESILIENCE AS AN EDUCATION LEADER?

Habits play a crucial role in shaping resilience for education leaders, as they form the foundation of how you react, adapt, and persist in all situations. As you navigate the extreme unpredictability of a job that demands your utmost clarity of mind and complete focus, your habits will provide you with a calm, predictable foundation for ways of thinking and acting that require almost no bandwidth to engage. As with the *Habits of Resilient Educators* (Prendergast & Lee, 2024) book, you will focus on building psychological capital, a practice supported by research on positive psychology, to support your ability to withstand change and uncertainty, become proactive, and develop a sense of control amidst chaos. Intentionally mastering skills, for example, around the habit of setting boundaries (Chapter 1) will empower you to apply healthy responses in demanding situations without almost any cognitive demand, easing your brain's levels of stress and protecting your attention for more impactful tasks such as casting an ambitious vision for your community (Chapter 3). You'll experience the opportunity within these chapters to draw connections across the habits, recognizing that becoming an expert in the art of seeking feedback and applying it to your personal and professional growth (Chapter 8) will amplify your efforts to develop the habit of checking your blind spots (Chapter 4) to ensure you improve at predicting how your community may react to new initiatives or ideas. Each of these habits has been carefully selected to support your growth at any stage of your career and to be revisited throughout your career as an iterative cycle of continuous personal improvement. As author Clear (2018) shared in *Atomic Habits*, "Habits are the compound interest of personal improvement" (p. 118). As you engage in the interactive activities within these chapters, you are investing small moments of your time and energy toward your broader goals of succeeding as a leader in education, and your daily efforts will multiply into a greater impact on both your well-being and the effect your leadership may have on the students and families in your school.

HOW TO USE THIS BOOK

Perhaps you find yourself reading this book at the start of your career as an education leader, or maybe you are well into your journey and seeking renewal and inspiration to offset the stressors and challenges around you. No matter the case, this book offers learning opportunities and fresh ideas applicable in any setting and for any individual. Though organized in a sequential manner, the chapters need not be explored to have an effect. Rather, the habits within these chapters are best understood as a web of practices and mindsets that intersect across and throughout the environments and scenarios you lead. As a result, consider each of the chapters and determine your ideal learning journey based on your needs and goals. You may explore habits based on the time of the school year when you are most likely to apply them or as a deep dive during a school holiday to gain insight into where each habit might be applied across your work. Without question, the concepts in the book are deeply amplified when explored in a setting with others: coach, mentor, fellow leaders, professional learning network, etc. For example, the opportunity to implement activities within each chapter will be enhanced with reflection conversations, bringing diverse perspectives and experiences to your personal approach. Regardless of how, when, and with whom you embark on the learning journey, prepare to grow and invest in your resilience as a leader so you may better serve your community!

In **Chapter 1**, you will begin your journey toward resilience by studying the merit of creating personal and professional boundaries as a leader. You will also learn strategies to clarify priorities; determine healthy boundaries across different environments and roles; and communicate with others around the "why," "who," and "how" these boundaries will ensure effective school leadership.

In **Chapter 2**, you'll explore how leaders who can sustain a high level of function in their professional lives often invest equally in nurturing a healthy personal life. This chapter presents practices and strategies to identify all aspects of one's identity, develop routines that balance personal and professional pursuits, and connect a leader's investment in their overall well-being to their impact on the students they serve.

Chapter 3 examines the habit of long-range *vision casting*. You'll explore the integration of data use, the practice of zeroing in on your purpose as a leader as it pertains to leading the school's vision, the crucial need to foster hope for the community, and many other leader actions that not only streamline your efforts but amplify your impact.

Chapter 4 centers on the habit of recognizing and addressing *blind spots* as a leader. It will introduce explicit practices such as identifying implicit biases, applying the concept of blind spots toward crucial leadership priorities, and building the most effective staff to achieve your highest outcomes for students.

In **Chapter 5**, you'll delve into a study of efficient, impactful practices for becoming a lead learner in your system. Practices and ideas will be presented around prioritizing *must know* information and strategically involving team members in the learning, reflecting on stakeholder behaviors across a consciousness/competence matrix, determining effective support actions, building leader credibility, and becoming an authentic activator of learning in your school or district.

In **Chapter 6**, you'll investigate how leaders may be at risk for inadvertently allowing a slow, gentle decline in expectations of their community and how that can have devastating cumulative effects. This chapter will provide strategies for building team maturity and understanding around the causes and effects of adult expectations, examine the effect of martyrdom in a school setting, and offer tools for *giving away the work* so others may become equal owners of the impact.

Chapter 7 will lead you on a journey toward effective use of data as a leader. You will learn strategies around using the data sources to *get curious*, seek powerful practices, identify sources of excellence to replicate, determine who and what needs attention for support, and continuously communicate with stakeholders the connection between data and instruction.

Chapter 8 addresses the key characteristics of feedback for education leaders, specifically examining the importance of seeking feedback for leaders in pursuit of their professional and community growth. You'll gain unique strategies for soliciting feedback and utilizing it to accelerate personal impact as a leader and connect feedback to overall school culture.

Chapter 9 will establish that leaders cannot have the fullest impact on their schools without comprehensive support from a network of mentors and coaches, fellow leaders, and the greater education community. You'll gain strategies for determining the type of networks that serve individual needs, how to build them, and practices for intentionally leveraging their value to foster your continuous growth as an education leader.

Chapter 10 culminates your study of the habits by examining how to skillfully navigate change as a leader. Building on the skills and mindsets developed across each of the other habits, you will develop approaches toward leading and managing change that empower you to confidently guide your community toward a vision of utmost success for every stakeholder.

Throughout this book, you will also experience practical stories from educational leaders, opportunities to apply your learning in the Pause and Reflect sections, and opportunities for journaling and reflection at the end of each chapter.

TAKE YOURSELF ON A PERSONAL GROWTH JOURNEY

As you begin the book, you will notice an early emphasis on the habit of investing in yourself. We invite you to embrace this mindset throughout every chapter as you create time and space to reflect, understand, and apply the practices within each habit. While much of your work as a leader inherently positions you to be the caretaker of those around you, without feeling fulfilled and healthy yourself, your efforts to support the teachers, families, and students in your community will further drain your precious energy reserves and put you at risk for ultimately being unable to take care of yourself, let alone of others. Thus, consider the learning experiences in this book as an entry point into the mindsets and practices that you may apply on a daily basis throughout your career to nourish your personal well-being and your professional capacity to lead. Rather than isolate self-care's personal and professional aspects, the habits you will study are situated at the intersection of the two. For example, as you learn the habit of utilizing data as a leader, you will not only apply practices that foster efficient data analysis to understand the effect of academic learning initiatives but you will also apply the habit of gathering data to inform how you interpret interpersonal interactions with those in your community. As such, you will understand that data may support your ability to be realistically optimistic in even the most challenging situations, a mindset recognized as an attribute of resilient individuals who navigate uncertainty with confidence and control. This is but one example of the myriad ways in which each of the habits applies to your work as an instructional leader and your own personal well-being. You deserve the time and space to learn these skills, and by investing in a conscious effort to apply them routinely, you will grow as a leader and amplify your positive impact on those you serve.

> *Without feeling fulfilled and healthy yourself, your efforts to support the teachers, families, and students in your community will further drain your precious energy reserves and put you at risk for ultimately being unable to take care of yourself, let alone of others.*

COLLABORATE WITH A MENTOR, COACH, OR PROFESSIONAL LEARNING COHORT

In Chapter 9, "Don't Travel Alone," you will study the habit of developing a thriving network of individuals and groups who may nourish your growth and support you in times of uncertainty. Before you reach that chapter, consider the opportunity to engage in your learning experience around all of the habits in collaboration with others. By partnering with a colleague, seeking a trusted mentor or coach, or perhaps gathering a group of fellow leaders to study the habits together, you will find that your learning grows exponentially. Surrounded by the fresh perspectives of others with backgrounds and experiences distinct from your own, each chapter's specific activities will become much more meaningful. Further, by partnering with a peer who may serve as a personal *accountability partner*, you will benefit from the effect of feeling motivated to uphold expectations for someone else who is counting on you to share the experience with you. There is no recipe for a perfect collaboration method around the book's content, but without question, this book is well-suited to being studied in partnership with others.

GET READY, SET YOUR INTENTIONS, AND GO IMPROVE!

MY LEARNING INTENTIONS FOR READING THIS BOOK ARE...
1.
2.
3.

Build Boundaries, Not Walls

Monique, a middle school principal beginning her third year, sat in her office and felt her heart begin to race. There were emotionally charged parents outside yelling at the administrative assistant. Through the door she heard enough to know they were demanding to see the principal. In several minutes, Monique's leadership team would be arriving to begin their weekly language arts instructional rounds together. She winced, realizing these had already been postponed from the previous week when she had to cancel to support the Assistant Principal in a delicate student conflict that was likely to upset most of the teaching staff with its outcome. Monique wanted nothing more than to prioritize her instructional leadership, and yet she struggled to do so as she was constantly reacting to the emotional needs of others. Thinking about her goals of student academic growth and achievement in reading made the overwhelm grow even deeper. Her phone pinged, and a text from the administrative assistant appeared. Did she have time to see the frustrated parents? Did she remember that her leadership team was also waiting for her to do language arts instructional rounds? In a moment of clarity, Monique decided to send the parents home and schedule a meeting with them after school. She called in her leadership team and let them know that instructional rounds were going to become a high priority. Moving forward, these would not be interrupted unless it was a true emergency. Later, meeting with the upset parents after school, she realized that because she had allowed some time to pass before meeting with her, they were not as emotionally charged. In fact, everyone was calmer and able to discuss the student concerns more rationally. As she reflected on the drive home, Monique realized that by communicating some simple boundaries with staff and parents in this instance, she had arrived at a better outcome for everyone, including herself.

WHY HEALTHY BOUNDARIES IN LEADERSHIP MATTER

In the context of education, professional and personal boundaries are becoming an essential habit for leaders to understand and maintain. Over the last decade, the pressure for school and district leaders to give more and more of their personal time has grown extremely prevalent. Technology has allowed leaders to become more accessible and to build relationships with stakeholders but has also created more access to work twenty-four hours a day, every day of the week. Through our extensive coaching and collaboration with schools and district leaders in action, we have observed patterns emerge that distinguished those education leaders who are becoming burnt out from those who continue to demonstrate job satisfaction. These fulfilled administrators have developed the skills of establishing, communicating, and maintaining boundaries in both their professional and personal lives. Boundaries are best described as the invisible lines that help us to effectively function in a manner that sustains our personal agency. Dr. Sharon Martin, a psychotherapist, describes how "with every relationship, personal or professional, comes the need for boundaries. Boundaries are the invisible lines that keep us physically and emotionally safe while effectively functioning. They govern what we are willing to do and not do, say and hear, and give and receive. Boundaries come in many forms." (2018).

Boundaries are best described as the invisible lines that help us to effectively function in a manner that sustains our personal agency.

Despite being widely recognized as an important practice for leaders (Weiss et al., 2018), the habit of setting healthy boundaries is not commonly discussed in educational leadership circles or journals. Rather, in the field of education, leaders (like teachers and others working in schools), may find themselves susceptible to a societal perception that they are expected to meet the needs of their entire community at all times—even at the cost of their own well-being. Further, education leaders may be attracted to the work because of the profound potential for being rewarded by helping others. Education is a profession known to draw the interest of individuals who aspire to impact the lives of others and to have a positive influence on society by shaping the futures of young people. By the very nature of the work, educators are often appropriately categorized as "servant leaders." With this prevalent mindset grounded in giving toward others, the profession is also at risk for positioning leaders as those who are easy to take advantage of by demanding unusually high outputs of time, attention to the needs of others, and even personal resources. Applying boundaries—a form of limits on external influences that serve to protect your needs—may feel unnatural or counterintuitive for leaders whose personal beliefs are grounded in taking care of others before themselves. However, learning to consistently and effectively apply boundaries serves to protect the capacity for fully giving love, attention, care, and expertise to a leader's community. Without them, no one is humanly capable of meeting all of the needs of every single stakeholder and burnout is inevitable.

Boundaries for all leaders are a critical habit that must be prioritized to ensure preservation of mental health, utmost effectiveness as a leader, and capacity to influence utmost high levels of student learning in classrooms. However, administrators, like many other professionals, may hold misconceptions about the purpose of defining and utilizing boundaries in the workplace. Consider the following characteristics that define what boundaries can, and cannot, offer school and district leaders for application in their setting (Figure 1.1).

FIGURE 1.1 ● Characteristics of Boundaries

WHAT BOUNDARIES ARE . . .	WHAT BOUNDARIES ARE NOT . . .
Boundaries allow you to prioritize your professional and personal needs and time.	Boundaries are not intended to control others' time.
Boundaries are a gate that allow those who are more responsible to gain more access to you.	Boundaries are not intended to control others' actions.
Boundaries allow for healthy communication.	Boundaries are not used to shut others' opinions or voices down.
Boundaries help to prioritize and protect your professional and personal goals.	Boundaries are not used to dictate others' goals.
Boundaries protect your happiness.	Boundaries do not stop others from acting irresponsibly.

Pause and Reflect

Read and reflect on the characteristics of boundaries in Figure 1.1 while responding to these questions.

Which of the statements from Figure 1.1 align most closely to your own *positive* experiences with boundary-setting (either using boundaries yourself or experiencing boundaries set by another individual)? Why do you believe that to be true?

_____

_____

_____

_____

_____

LET BOUNDARIES BECOME YOUR SUPERPOWER!

Utilizing boundaries is not typically encountered in traditional leadership development courses, nor in educator certification programs. Further, the act of defining a boundary around one's personal needs, goals, interests, or preferences may feel downright uncomfortable to some. Establishing a boundary first requires understanding how it feels when your subconscious beliefs and assumptions about right and wrong are affronted and why those feelings occur in each situation. Examples of boundaries that may be crossed might include intrusions on your time, a conflict with your internal expectations about how a project should be accomplished, or a colleague consistently taking advantage of your perceived willingness to take on more of the difficult tasks at work. While your role is one that involves supporting others, setting limits is both necessary and healthy. Creating a boundary is not about making yourself unavailable; it's about managing your time and energy so you can be at your best for those whom you lead. When faced with an experience that feels like an intrusion on your unspoken expectations, a boundary can help! Specific practices that enable the creation of healthy boundaries can include the following:

1. Clarifying your priorities: When you are certain about what must happen to ensure success (for any type of scenario),

you can better ascertain what will hinder progress and more easily say "no" to those requests or tasks.

2. Communicating directly and kindly: Setting boundaries by telling others "no" can cause feelings of guilt. With clear communication as to why you are not able to accede to a request you avoid misunderstandings or assumptions and establish fair, clear expectations.

3. Setting boundaries before intrusions occur: You may notice patterns in your interactions with others wherein they seem to make assumptions about how and when to interact with you. Preemptively establishing boundaries that will diminish these instances, such as clear blocks and open spaces on your calendar for when you're free for certain things, can fend off unintended dissonance from having to decline meetings or appear uninterested in collaborating.

While your role is one that involves supporting others, setting limits is both necessary and healthy. Creating a boundary is not about making yourself unavailable; it's about managing your time and energy so you can be at your best for those whom you lead.

Consider this scenario about VaShawn, an experienced Deputy Superintendent and former principal who ascribes to the belief that his purpose as an educator is to help all students achieve their potential, no matter what cost:

VaShawn left the meeting with the team of middle school principals with a deep knot in his stomach. The discussion had circled for two hours around the data suggesting the Emergent Bilingual population of students in the district were not growing academically from year to year; worse, they were declining in achievement for the third year in a row. The school leaders identified dozens of contributing reasons for the disturbing data, and VaShawn countered them with a long list of solutions he had prepared in advance of the meeting. Leaving that day, not one principal had agreed to adopt any of his solutions. He was adamant that he would never force the principals to do something against their will, but he was equally certain the family engagement program he had designed was one of the best solutions to the challenges at hand. Begrudgingly, he now landed on the notion that he would have to spearhead the initiative through his office and not burden the principals with his ideals. He felt the uncomfortable sensation of resentment growing in his conscience against the principals he began to judge as lazy and apathetic, yet it would be inappropriate to confront their

(Continued)

Chapter 1 • Build Boundaries, Not Walls 13

resistance directly. As he arrived home, he spent much of the evening venting his irritation to his partner. The next day, he initiated the first steps toward launching the family engagement project on his own.

While VaShawn is a talented and effective leader in many ways, he's apprehensive at establishing several types of boundaries in his work with his team of school principals, and this places him at risk for adverse outcomes that may cause his own well-being and job satisfaction to suffer. For example, the problem being discussed with the leaders was a set of data that belonged to everyone in the room, not just a few schools and not just VaShawn. His approach to offer a selection of solutions to the administrators was honorable, reasonable, and efficient. VaShawn also arrived at the meeting with an assumption about the outcome he desired to achieve: the leaders would assume responsibility for the data and elect the most effective interventions to adopt and implement in response. For VaShawn to effectively achieve his goals for an action plan, protect his own need to relentlessly pursue what is best for the district's students, and respect the rights of the group of principals to preserve their integrity and lead their buildings according to their expertise, he could shift the experience altogether by deploying his superpower boundaries! Consider the examples in Figure 1.2 describing ways VaShawn might use boundaries to achieve the environment most likely to ensure successful outcomes.

FIGURE 1.2 ● Boundary Examples

DESIRED STATE	EFFECTIVE USE OF BOUNDARIES TO ACHIEVE THE DESIRED STATE
VaShawn and the principals collaboratively develop an action plan for interventions in response to the data.	Clear definition of roles at the onset of the meeting. Implement meeting norms with the group to ensure equal participation, collective responsibility, and shared outcomes.
Principals retain agency over their respective school sites and implementation plans.	VaShawn preemptively determines a few *nonnegotiables* as well as explicit opportunities for individual choice.
VaShawn sustains his personal purpose of adapting to the current environment and responding effectively to meet the needs of all students.	VaShawn leads the meetings with frequent reiterations of the district mission and vision—the "why" for all decisions made. At the meeting conclusion, VaShawn communicates a long-range framework for implementation that incorporates regular feedback cycles from principals.

Pause and Reflect

As you journey through this chapter and those coming afterward, reflect on your own shifts within unique leadership experiences. These reflection questions may guide your examination of when boundaries may have been a superpower you could have deployed to achieve your desired state!

What assumptions or hidden expectations do you hold of others as you initiate a new decision, initiative, program, or other action as a leader? Why might others need to know those expectations?

_____

_____

_____

_____

_____

What emotions might you experience if not all of the stakeholders involved in your next project or initiative respond in accordance with your expectations?

_____

_____

_____

_____

_____

How might defining explicit boundaries for yourself and for others *before* beginning the project or initiative foster success for everyone involved?

_____

_____

_____

_____

_____

REAP THE REWARDS OF HEALTHY BOUNDARY-SETTING

It's crucial when learning to improve your habit of boundary-setting that you understand the different types of boundaries, how they might appear in the education setting, and the risks and rewards you may incur if you do, or do not, apply them. We created Figure 1.3 to guide you in this endeavor.

FIGURE 1.3 ● Types of Boundaries

TYPE OF BOUNDARY	BOUNDARY VIOLATION EXAMPLES	IMPACT WHEN BOUNDARIES ARE NOT APPLIED	BENEFITS OF APPLYING THIS TYPE OF BOUNDARY
Emotional Boundaries: What, where, and how much a person shares their emotional life and how your own and others' emotional needs are handled.	Staff expect you to always know, without being told, what they need and attend to those needs so that they feel supported when managing student behavior.	Leaders feel as though they are constantly disappointing their stakeholders, leading to frustration and diminished self-worth.	Clearly sharing with teachers that you cannot know their needs unless they are shared explicitly, then affirming efforts to share needs with positive support.
Material Boundaries: Treatment of possessions and property and how possessions and property are shared or withheld.	Colleagues assume because you are an administrator that you earn a substantial income and should always cover the bill for social outings.	Conceding to others' expectations when it comes to finances easily harms your personal budget and can lead to resentment toward others.	When a boundary is established, respect is formed and everyone involved is able to enjoy being together without hidden judgments or assumptions.
Time Boundaries: How you relate to your own and others' time and how time-related needs and preferences are treated.	Parents aren't sure how you spend your time and draw conclusions you are always readily available, becoming disgruntled when you don't respond to their needs as immediately as they are presented.	Giving your precious time to anyone who demands it and at the moment they demand it ensures you will never have enough time to attend to the demanding work of leading the entire school toward its vision.	Creating systems and structures, and then clearly sharing them and upholding them consistently, offers a healthy framework under which all stakeholders know the *rules* and can operate reasonably within them, thus you remain in control of your time.

TYPE OF BOUNDARY	BOUNDARY VIOLATION EXAMPLES	IMPACT WHEN BOUNDARIES ARE NOT APPLIED	BENEFITS OF APPLYING THIS TYPE OF BOUNDARY
Personal Limit Boundaries: How often you place your personal needs and desires as the last priority, making sacrifices of your time and effort predominantly to meet others' needs.	Your predecessor established the unwritten expectation that the principal should attend every single after-school activity, even traveling with student teams to events. Doing so means you have zero time for personal health pursuits, least of all your family.	Upholding high demands by others on your personal time for fear of disappointing stakeholders puts your own health at risk—both mental and physical—for being *hands on, mind on* beyond healthy levels for a job.	Ensuring meaningful engagements at some events as opposed to attending every single one shows stakeholders you care for the entire community, yet protects your nonwork time and models healthy work-life balance for your staff.
Social Boundaries: Alignment of your words and behavior with your values, and your responses to others when this alignment is violated.	Fellow administrators constantly disparage their district bosses and the superintendent whenever you are together, bringing down your optimistic attitude and calling into question your commitment to the work.	Allowing those around you to control the narrative of every conversation in a negative or disparaging direction drains your happiness, diminishes your confidence in your own leaders, and fractures trust at all levels.	Defining the impact of such behavior with peers informs them that their actions are harming you. Withholding your presence from their conversations preserves your mental attitude and sustains focus on areas that bring hope, joy, and optimism.

HOW SCHOOL STAKEHOLDERS BENEFIT FROM LEADERS' BOUNDARIES

While setting boundaries is generally a healthy practice, there are unique circumstances through which to consider the impact of boundaries differently for different members of your community. For example, setting a clear boundary with fellow administrators that you don't wish to spend time disparaging your supervisors together is likely to be unnecessary with the teachers in your school. Modeling boundaries with parents around how they are able to set time to meet with you, however, is likely a fantastic opportunity to model healthy boundary practices for those same teachers to use in their own practice. In this section, you'll examine strategies and practices for setting healthy boundaries with the following groups:

- your leadership team
- classroom educators whom you lead
- students and families

Consider the intersections and distinct practices throughout each section as you look for opportunities to amplify your own growth journey within this habit and look forward to opportunities for deepening this work while practicing other habits such as upholding high expectations for all and the art of getting feedback.

MODELING HEALTHY BOUNDARIES WITH BUILDING LEADERSHIP TEAMS

Modeling boundaries with your leadership team helps demonstrate what good leaders say, do, and how we respond to others. As an education leader, you set the tone for your team's culture, so demonstrating how to establish and maintain boundaries is key. Start by being transparent about your own boundaries—for example, let your team know when you're unavailable for non-urgent matters, such as during family time or dedicated focus blocks. This helps others understand that it's okay to prioritize personal time without guilt. Another strategy is to be clear about meeting expectations—set agendas, keep discussions focused, and honor agreed-upon end times to respect everyone's schedules. Encourage team members to take regular breaks and respect their need for personal time, especially during high-stress periods. By modeling these practices with consistency, your team will understand their importance and be more likely to apply the approaches themselves.

Another area where leaders have an important opportunity to model healthy boundaries is in how you navigate experiences that are out of your control. For example, it is inevitable that in an era of great change someone will dislike any change you or the district makes and they will become angry. It is in those moments that you may want to just make people happy or become a people pleaser. However, not maintaining healthy professional boundaries in your response may briefly allow that one negative nagging voice to be happy, but you run the risk of violating the vision, goals, and needs of the rest of your staff and students. Further, you may find it comforting to process difficult experiences by verbalizing your frustrations or disappointments with others as a way of fostering relatability and empathy. The absence of a boundary around how you communicate and with whom may invite your stakeholders to feel equally negative about an experience or, worse, convey your opinions to others as though they are concrete information. In the face of disruption, change, or uncertainty, support your team and your own needs instead by establishing space and time for courageous conversations, inviting others to have a healthy conversation so they can feel seen, heard, and valued while establishing those clear boundaries of how we talk about district decisions, staff, and students.

SETTING HEALTHY BOUNDARIES WITH CLASSROOM EDUCATORS

Relationships between principals, educators, and school support staff can be polarizing at times. A principal plays many distinct roles as a building leader, which can complicate the delicate dance of creating healthy boundaries with school staff. Principals operate with a collaborative stance, a coaching stance, and a directive stance. However, they must also build trusting relationships with all staff members regardless of the role they are playing. "There is not a singular action that will lead to developing a trusting relationship, but rather multiple actions over an extended period to earn that trust" (Medor, 2019, p. 1). In other words, building relationships through a variety of actions with healthy boundaries takes time.

One action step that helps establish clarity and trust in professional relationships is a Clarifying Roles and Tasks workflow chart. This chart helps educators and principals determine who is responsible for tasks that may arise. The key is to clarify the roles of each task and identify which person is the key responsibility holder. By articulating each of these areas, team members are empowered to understand when they are expected to take action and each individual is aware of where the others are focusing their effort. These boundaries, or established rules of engagement, instill the confidence for all to move forward and trust that the goals are clear and other areas are not being ignored or left undone.

These boundaries, or established rules of engagement, instill the confidence for all to move forward and trust that the goals are clear and other areas are not being ignored or left undone.

Pause and Reflect

Use this chart to brainstorm specific ways that the roles different individuals might be defined when a group or team is focusing on different day-to-day tasks. Examples of tasks have been provided (though you may choose to create your own), and the subsequent columns provide space to journal your ideas.

Sample Clarifying Roles and Tasks Workflow

TASK	PRINCIPAL	EDUCATOR
Communication with students about before and after school procedures		
Communicating when a child is bullied		
Communicating academic celebrations		
Communicating PLC agenda		
Communicating expectations around implementing the new curriculum		

TASK	PRINCIPAL	EDUCATOR

SETTING HEALTHY BOUNDARIES WITH STUDENTS AND FAMILIES

Boundaries are an essential element of trust. When you have no boundaries, it leaves the other person guessing what the guardrails are (Lofgren, 2021). It is evident that in all relationships within the school that leaders must work hard to develop trust. Students and families come from many backgrounds and may have faced lots of trauma and overwhelm over the last decade. Now more than ever it is essential for leaders to help clearly define the guardrails or boundaries that will help all parties effectively function. We have more trust in those who help us by articulating the guardrails. For example, consider Monique's successful experience establishing a clear and simple boundary with the help of her administrative assistant to always ask parents to come back later in the day when she has availability on her calendar. Consider the merit of the formal structure for this boundary that adds further clarity for all involved: create a standing open time such as *office hours* exclusively to handle any parent or student challenges that may have arisen earlier in the day. Such a practice can serve to provide those clear guardrails so that parents and students can't constantly march into your office and command your attention at any time of their choosing. In the following chart, consider more opportunities that could steal time from your calendar and how you will want to handle those. Providing these guardrails to each member of your community will help build a trusting atmosphere.

Pause and Reflect

Use the chart to identify possible challenges and plans for boundaries when managing the relationships of students, families, and the school.

POSSIBLE CHALLENGE	DESIRED OUTCOME	BOUNDARY: GUARDRAILS TO SUPPORT THE DESIRED OUTCOME
Example: A teacher persistently arrives to team meetings several minutes late, commonly reporting being *stuck* with students after school.	All staff respect the sanctity of team meetings and one another's time by being punctual and prepared. Staff don't consume extra time with you to catch up on missed information from arriving to meetings late.	1. All-staff reminder of the purpose of punctuality for all team gatherings. 2. Individual conference with the specific teacher describing clear expectations and the impact of their behavior on you and the team. 3. As needed, prompt emails addressing the missed expectations following the communication, ensuring they are aware you *inspect what you expect*.

POSSIBLE CHALLENGE	DESIRED OUTCOME	BOUNDARY: GUARDRAILS TO SUPPORT THE DESIRED OUTCOME

As you develop your skills at identifying, utilizing, and upholding good boundaries, remember "Boundaries are only effective when we set and enforce them with ourselves and others. These are the rules, and we have to be willing to accept the consequences of enforcing them, because the consequences are far greater than when we don't. We are not victims of our circumstances. Boundaries give us the power to choose and the responsibility to decide" (Cloud, 2013, p. 7). Putting the habit of using boundaries to work is an investment not only in yourself, but in the impact you may have on the students and staff in your school.

The Big Ideas

In this chapter, you explored the idea that identifying and applying boundaries in your personal and professional life can be a crucial practice toward ensuring that you are able to bring your best self to the work you want to do: elevate learning for every single student in your school. As you begin to move through forthcoming chapters, recall how you connected the strategies described herein to the people and structures in your current role. Chapter 1 laid the foundation to understand the importance of boundaries in creating realistic expectations of yourself and for others and shared ideas for communicating this intent across each of your school or district's different stakeholder groups. Prepare to examine the intersection of these practices and the range of skills you will develop in the chapters ahead on your journey toward becoming a resilient leader.

Let's Reflect

1. What new ideas have extended your prior knowledge on the concept of boundaries to support your professional growth and development?

_____

_____

_____

2. Who might you collaborate with as a learning partner or for additional support in your practice around utilizing boundaries to foster your professional and personal well-being?

_____

_____

_____

3. What strategy from Chapter 1 might you first apply to your daily work? How will you utilize the chapter content to gauge your progress thereafter?

_____

_____

_____

What's Next?

In Chapter 2, you'll examine the importance of investing energy and time into being fulfilled in all areas of your life, rather than being overly consumed by the demands of your role as a leader. By learning about boundaries first, you'll be equipped to apply the explicit strategies found throughout Chapter 2, such as effectively using feedback, as you investigate skills in leading the learning in your school or district. Look to Chapter 2 for ways to use boundaries to help foster an identity that is robustly developed with passions, hobbies, and relationships. But don't forget to check back to Chapter 1 for cross-application possibilities and watch your growth and impact as a resilient leader multiply!

Fill Your Bucket First

The Habit of Self-Care

Josefina, a veteran elementary principal with twenty-nine years in the same district, sat at her desk, staring quietly at her to-do list on the computer in her office. She was exhausted, overwhelmed, and honestly burnt out from the years of service in education. Josefina loved the profession and believed in her staff, students, and families, but over the years, she set her own emotions aside and focused her energy almost exclusively on her community. She knew her staff was also feeling overwhelmed and burnt out. She had just thrown a surprise appreciation event to show them her deep appreciation for their hard work. She and her husband had spent the entire weekend with the PTSA decorating the foyer and school for the special day. Josefina had gathered gift cards, brought in a massage and spa team, catered breakfast, and hosted a red-carpet event for her entire staff. However, even though she found great joy in supporting her staff and giving the gift of appreciation to them, she was still feeling uninspired, hopeless, and persistently frustrated. Josefina met with her leadership coach and shared her troubling emotions. As the two discussed the many challenges that leaders face, it became evident that while Josefina had worked hard to invest in her staff's well-being with grati-tude and kindness, she also forgot to invest in herself. She cringed when her coach asked her, "How do you ensure that your cup remains full so that you can continue to pour into others?" Josefina's eyes welled with tears as she recognized an important truth: amidst her myriad efforts to support her staff and students, she had no time or energy to take care of herself. With this realization came another: if she was not the best version of herself, she could not expect her community to ever achieve their very best.

WHY SELF-CARE
MATTERS FOR LEADERS

In 2006, Carol McCloud wrote a best-selling children's book, *Have You Filled a Bucket Today?* Carol's book continues to be used in schools across the nation. This charming story teaches that everybody carries an invisible bucket to hold all their good thoughts and feelings about themselves. Having a full bucket makes you feel good about yourself while having an empty bucket leaves you with uncomfortable feelings (Peaceful Schools, 2013). The book centers on being kind to others and investing in their happiness, neglecting to teach another important lesson: our own happiness is equally, if not more, important. Education leaders often overextend themselves and pour out all their physical, mental, emotional, and even financial resources to support others, leaving their own *buckets* depleted and empty. In Chapter 1, you explored the importance of developing healthy boundaries around your personal needs to achieve well-being. One such boundary may be understanding how an imbalance of meeting others' needs more often than your own cultivates exhaustion and, at worst, the emotional state of burnout—a complete lack of desire to continue in a job that you may have once truly loved. Though boundaries provide us with a means for eliminating unhealthy intrusions and negative influences, they don't refill our empty energy reserves or reignite our passions. For that, we must pour back into ourselves and fill our own bucket.

Education leaders often overextend themselves and pour out all their physical, mental, emotional, and even financial resources to support others, leaving their own buckets depleted and empty.

In another best seller, *The Five Love Languages* by Chapman (2010), the author states that we must be aware of the types of activities or actions that fill our own *cup*. Chapman (2010) uses the analogy that we cannot pour from an empty cup or teapot. However, there seems to be a prevalent belief in education leadership that servant leadership is the most important or the only quality in a good leader. While servant leadership is an impactful approach, when taken too far, the leader may risk losing their identity or becoming overwhelmed by excessive focus on others' needs. Leaders may find themselves striving for sainthood, not servanthood, failing to give themselves permission to pause and recognize their limits. No matter a leader's experience level, meeting all the needs of our districts, schools, staff, students, and communities is fundamentally impossible. Such aspirations become even more unrealistic in the presence of stress, overwhelm, and burnout.

Regardless, in countless working environments, education leaders are encouraged to work long hours and are frequently told, "Well, this was the job you signed up for." A culture that rewards workaholics is toxic and not sustainable. K. J. Patel (2020), author of *Burning Bright,* dedicated an entire book to examining the impact of such cultures and defining the necessary antidote: the habit of self-care. Patel states, "In our fast-paced lives, stressors abound. Work pressures, technology overload, and the constant stream of emails contribute to feelings of overwhelm. Loneliness compounds these challenges, leaving us less able to unwind and find solace. As a result, anxiety and depression have become an epidemic affecting countless individuals" (2020, p. 143). When leaders are overwhelmed and exhausted, such as Josefina in the earlier story, they cannot bring their best version of themselves to work, making this challenging role even more difficult. Spending time focusing on self-care and ensuring your own bucket or cup is full is your job. As leaders, we must focus on the physical, mental, emotional, and spiritual aspects of life as we promote and model health and wellness to our staff and students. Before examining explicit strategies for meaningful self-care, let's identify exactly what defines self-care (or, metaphorically, *filling your bucket*) and what it is not (Figure 2.1).

FIGURE 2.1 ● Characteristics of Self-Care

WHAT SELF-CARE IS . . .	WHAT SELF-CARE IS NOT . . .
It's about intentionally taking time to prioritize your physical, mental, and emotional well-being; it's about recognizing your needs and actively addressing them	Prioritizing the well-being of others before yourself
Acknowledging and processing your feelings, seeking support when needed, and practicing self-compassion	Armoring up, numbing, and ignoring your feelings Trying to be a superhuman and remaining in your silo or cone of silence
Engaging in activities that promote health and relaxation, such as exercise, meditation, getting enough sleep, and eating nourishing meals	An excuse to escape from responsibilities or challenges
An activity or simple pause in your day that allows your mind, body, and emotions to rejuvenate or provides the physical or mental break needed to continue being healthy and productive throughout your day and life	An elaborate, expensive, or complicated event or activity

Pause and Reflect

Considering the characteristics of self-care, answer these questions:

REFLECTIVE PRACTICE QUESTIONS	MY CURRENT REALITY	WHAT IS ONE BEHAVIOR YOU WOULD LIKE TO INCORPORATE INTO YOUR DAY DURING THE NEXT WEEK THAT WOULD SUPPORT YOUR WELL-BEING?
What are your current habits of filling your bucket or practicing self-care?		
What do you notice *mentally* when you give yourself permission to pause and provide what you need to refill your bucket?		
What do you notice *physically* when you give yourself permission to pause and gather what you need to refill your bucket?		
What do you notice *socially* when you give yourself permission to pause and provide yourself with what you need to refill your bucket?		

SELF-CARE CANNOT BE SUPERFICIAL

As attention to leader attrition, like teacher attrition, increases across the globe, the term "self-care" has perhaps increased in presence at almost equal rates. In the absence of systemic improvement, the prolonged, profound stressors found in education systems—such as the extraordinary demands on school to achieve superhuman feats of accelerated student learning with no more time in the typical day than before—leaders are advised to take better care of themselves physically and emotionally. Fundamental to the likelihood of these well-intended recommendations having any effect is a need to recognize what you personally need to feel fulfilled and confident in your work. No amount of exercise classes or accolades from supervisors will address your diminished well-being if the treatments only address the symptoms, not the cause, of your personal state. If your work and personal lives feel out of balance, for example, consider reflecting on the areas of your work life that are threatening your well-being and causing the distorted relationship. As you examine each of the habits throughout the book, you will gain insights and opportunities for navigating these persistent stressors in ways that foster resilience, the ultimate healthy outcome of effective self-care.

If your work and personal lives feel out of balance, for example, consider reflecting on the areas of your work life that are threatening your well-being and causing the distorted relationship.

PERMISSION TO PAUSE

Taking time to fill your bucket and focus on a specific area of self-care is not selfish but truly helps build resiliency. Reflecting on what is working well and what changes you must make is half the battle. Self-care is and should be very personalized. Self-care that benefits your friends, spouse, children, or colleagues may or may not require the same need or in the same way. However, reflecting on your needs and listening to what others might notice about your needs is a terrific place to start.

We might avoid filling our own bucket because we feel exhausted or overwhelmed, or experience decision fatigue. Prioritizing self-care amidst a sea of initiatives may feel like one more thing to do. Consider, however, how prioritizing filling your bucket and focusing on one self-care area is similar to following the directions from flight attendants when traveling in tumultuous conditions on planes. Passengers are instructed to put on their oxygen masks before helping others get their masks on. These directions intend to help with the basic need of life: breathing.

Filling your bucket and knowing the areas of self-care you might need to give yourself permission to pause and focus on is no different. To be a resilient leader and not suffer from burnout, we must treat self-care as a need, not a want. Investing in your self-care now means you are investing in long-term health and well-being. Now, let's explore the various types of self-care and consider how each domain intersects to support the others.

BUILDING UPON BOUNDARIES: THE DOMAINS OF SELF-CARE

Social media and sophisticated marketing campaigns in the wellness industry have exhausted us with the phrase "self-care." Expensive self-indulgence pampering practices, bubble baths, massages, and skin and hair products are now equated with looking out for our well-being. For some people, this has led to the phrase "self-care" taking on a negative connotation of self-indulgence, rather than the important habit that it is truly meant to be. Thus, we decided to call this habit "bucket-filling," as we recognize the cognitive dissonance around naming self-care as a powerful habit that education leaders must attend to. Regardless, the term "self-care," as defined by the World Health Organization (WHO), is the ability of an individual to promote and maintain health, prevent disease, and cope with illness and disability with or without the support of a healthcare provider (2024). According to the Health Coach Institute (2023), there are numerous distinct domains of self-care. For the education leader, we will focus on four: emotional, physical, mental, and social.

Pause and Reflect

As you read the characteristics of the domains of self-care, return here to journal what you notice about the presence of alignment between the self-care domains and the types of boundaries described in Chapter 1.

_____

_____

_____

_____

_____

EMOTIONAL SELF-CARE

Emotional self-care includes pausing and noticing your feelings and emotions and permitting yourself to take deliberate action to attend to them. As leaders, we often support staff, students, families, and colleagues who express intense negative emotions. In our current culture, most education leaders encounter numerous negative and intense interactions with others every single day of the week. Taking an emotional pause for yourself as you process others' negative moods may be an essential bucket-filling strategy you must consciously implement into your daily routine. Unfortunately, emotional self-care is undervalued and potentially the most unattended area of the self-care domains. However, for education leaders to create a psychologically safe environment, they must be self-regulated and consistently attend to their own emotional needs before modeling, leading, or supervising others.

Here are some strategies to develop the habit of emotional self-care:

- Increase your GQ (Gratitude Quotient) by developing daily routines to help fight against apathy and negativity that you may be surrounded by. This is not about developing toxic positivity but authentically reflecting on your true gratitude for professional or personal things.
- Use a calm or meditation app to help calm your mind and body.
- Talk with a coach, counselor, or spiritual thought partner.
- Create a playlist of songs that help encourage, calm, and inspire you.
- Create a list of "I am" statements to help focus on your self-talk (e.g., I am strong and can do hard things).

PHYSICAL SELF-CARE

Physical self-care includes anything that impacts, improves, or maintains the health and wellness of your body. The health coaching industry has significantly increased within the last few years. In 2019, health coaching was a 2.9-billion-dollar industry, and it has now more than doubled, estimated to be over 6 billion in 2024 (Waite, 2024). When working with a health coach, five distinct areas are typically prioritized for setting goals to improve and maintain physical health and wellness. These six focus areas are physical exercise, eating healthy, balanced meals, sleep habits, staying hydrated, and attending regular healthcare appointments. These six areas of focus seem well-known, but we need to maintain our attention on these essential physical areas.

Educators often brag or consider it a badge of honor to skip meals, exercise, or sleep. Adult and child obesity has become a well-known national crisis. "From 1999–2000 through 2017–March 2020, US obesity prevalence increased from 30.5% to 41.9%" (National Center for Health Statistics, 2021). Therefore, focusing on one's physical health and wellness is worth investing time and resources. As leaders, we must evaluate how we are taking care of ourselves physically despite the demands of education.

Here are some strategies to develop the habit of physical self-care:

- Develop a habit of prioritizing when and what you are eating. Make lunch or eating while working a daily priority. Develop daily routines to pause and sit and slowly eat your food, whether a protein bar or a packed lunch.

- Get an alarm clock for your bedroom and leave your phone in the kitchen. When you go to your bedroom, allow yourself time to calm down. Your bedroom should be a sanctuary of rest, not an extension of your office.

- Bring a water bottle to work and set daily goals for how much you will drink.

- Create an exercise schedule and honor your appointments with yourself as you would an appointment with work.

- Schedule your annual health appointments when you know you will not have to reschedule or skip.

MENTAL SELF-CARE

Mental self-care is one of the domains that people tend to notice more quickly when compromising this area of focus. Some of the symptoms of a lack of mental self-care might be anxiety, lack of focus, physical and mental exhaustion, memory, decision fatigue, impatience, sadness, or frustration. Cognitive fatigue also quickly impacts our ability to show up regularly as the best versions of ourselves. We use phrases such as "crazy busy" and "crazy hot mess" to discuss mental well-being. However, we know that more mistakes are made when our brain operates in fight or flight mode versus being calm and able to make quick but good decisions that lead to positive outcomes. Most professionals know when they have hit their mental wall and recognize that mental self-care is of utmost importance when working in demanding careers. Making sure that you take time for your brain to get the mental self-care it needs allows you to remain in the calm mode versus the crazy mode. When our brains operate in calm mode, we are more effective and efficient with time and tasks we need to accomplish, even when facing a sea of initiatives and other people's *crazy hot messes*.

When our brains operate in calm mode, we are more effective and efficient with time and tasks we need to accomplish, even when facing a sea of initiatives and other people's crazy hot messes.

Here are some strategies to develop the habit of mental self-care:

- Read a book that helps you learn something new or allows you to escape from the mental overwhelm you may be experiencing.

- Carve time out for puzzles, adult coloring, yoga, and card games.

- Walk outside at the end of the workday or before bedtime.

- Listen to an encouraging or funny podcast to and from work.

- Hire a health/life coach to talk with regularly.

SOCIAL SELF-CARE

The human experience involves interpersonal connection. Social connections are essential and provide a sense of feeling valued, loved, and cared for. However, with the demands on education leaders, social self-care seems to be an area that gets put on the back burner. Long days at the office with intense cognitive demands create exhaustion and overwhelm. Often, the first thing we do when exhausted is isolate or remove social events from our calendars to meet the demands of our jobs.

Consequently, our lack of social self-care and connection with others may create isolation, sadness, and loneliness. Social self-care is a fundamental need and helps us create bonds with other people, building our sense of belonging. Social media has also become a challenge because although people may feel connected by scrolling, looking, and learning about their friends' and families' lives, it can actually have a negative effect on our sense of self and our social identity. "Unfortunately, connecting in the real world can be more challenging than ever. Increased technology use, telecom, and social media may keep us in constant digital contact. However, excess Internet use might also play a part in degrading our ability to connect more meaningfully" (Cherry, 2023, para. 2).

Here are some strategies to develop the habit of social self-care:

- Put your phone away for a few hours after work a few times a week. Make an effort to either meet up with some friends and eat dinner together or set aside a family or date night that is intentional to foster connection and relationship with those you care about and who care about you.

- Join a social club: pickleball, hiking, book, golf, or cooking class.
- Take your vacation days and plan a staycation with your friends and family. Take the time to simply focus on your relationships.
- Schedule lunch breaks or coffee breaks with your colleagues. Find a colleague you trust and build time into your week or month to meet with them without an agenda. Simply spend the time investing in the relationship.

Pause and Reflect

Use this chart to determine which activities bring you joy and restore your balance. Start small by choosing one self-care area that you would like to focus on in the next week.

SELF-CARE DOMAIN	CURRENT REALITY (HOW MIGHT THIS AREA IMPACT YOU POSITIVELY OR NEGATIVELY?)	STRATEGY TO TRY (IDENTIFY ONE STRATEGY TO HELP YOU IMPROVE YOUR SELF-CARE.)
Physical Self-Care		
Emotional Self-Care		
Mental Self-Care		
Social Self-Care		

INVESTING IN YOURSELF IS AN EQUAL INVESTMENT IN YOUR STAFF AND STUDENTS

As you explore the various domains of self-care and consider their application in practice, consider the experience of Tamara, an early-career principal who is grappling with the delicate balance of serving the needs of all of her stakeholders and simultaneously attending to her personal needs for self-care:

Tamara had spent five years working as an assistant principal under the guidance of an experienced leader whose effectiveness was heralded throughout the district. She observed as he regularly stayed at the school working until the early evening hours, attended nearly every single school activity no matter the location or time, and had often been known to miss being present for his own children's extracurricular events in order to "be visible" for the community of his school. She strived to match his seemingly endless energy for work, but even within a few years, she felt drained and resentful at her work for consuming her personal life. Now, as a new principal, she grappled with the model she wished to portray for her staff, students, and families. She wondered about the precedent she would set if she began immediately engaging at the same high levels as her former boss and the impact that would have on her long-range well-being versus the desire to show her community that she deeply cared about her students beyond their presence during the hours of a school day.

For Tamara, like all leaders striving toward servant leadership, there is a risk in always placing the needs of others before those of ourselves. However, recognizing the merit and valuable rewards of an investment into our own well-being as a leader is not exclusively self-serving. Consider these examples of different school stakeholders and how they are impacted when a leader intentionally prioritizes their well-being through the different self-care domains:

Pause and Reflect

STAKEHOLDER GROUP	EXAMPLE OF POSITIVE IMPACT WHEN A LEADER PRIORITIZES THEIR SELF-CARE	WHAT ADDITIONAL EXAMPLES OF POSITIVE OUTCOMES MIGHT YOU ENVISION AS YOU PRIORITIZE YOUR SELF-CARE?
Staff	As leaders prioritize their own physical self-care, they model the value of taking time to sustain healthy physical activities; this conveys to staff that they, too, are supported to balance their personal and professional life activities.	
Students	When leaders invest in mental self-care, they are more apt to be compassionate, empathetic, and supportive when navigating student behavioral challenges.	
Families	When leaders prioritize their emotional well-being through self-care, they are equipped to engage with all families in the school, free from negative emotional states that influence interpersonal relationships.	

The Big Ideas

Education leaders are at risk of wrapping up a great deal of their identity in their profession. Society also tends to support the mindset that educators should completely sacrifice their whole selves for the benefit of the school they serve. Conversely, leaders who can sustain a high level of function in their professional lives often invest equally in nurturing a healthy personal life. In doing so, they *fill their bucket* with passions, hobbies, activities, and pursuits that provide them with a foundational understanding that they are valued, competent, and worthy of others' care. When leaders don't fill their own bucket but rather associate their worthiness and personal identity as education leaders at the exclusion of all other characteristics, they risk experiencing substantial disappointment and insecurity when this identity is threatened. Today's educational environment challenges leaders with constant threats, and the leaders whose personal and professional lives are imbalanced are ill-equipped to manage their responses without negatively affecting the school's ecosystem and overall student learning. It is essential for today's school leaders to reflect on strategies that identify all aspects of one's identity, develop routines that balance personal and professional pursuits, and connect a leader's investment in their overall well-being to their impact on the students they serve.

Let's Reflect

1. What will likely be the most significant challenge to your growth in filling your bucket? What actions or beliefs do you need to take or change to overcome that challenge?

   _____

   _____

   _____

2. What areas of self-care within this chapter are you most excited to implement right away?

   _____

   _____

   _____

(Continued)

(Continued)

3. How do you plan to share with your friends, family, or staff what you have learned about filling your bucket? Who can you connect with as an accountability partner?

_____

_____

_____

What's Next?

Building upon what you have learned from Chapters 1 and 2, you are becoming equipped to deploy all of your superpowers to the utmost potential! With a deep foundation of strategies to protect and invest in yourself, the students and staff in your care will reap the rewards. Next, in Chapter 3, you will dive deeply into strategies to help you develop and maintain a vision for a school or district. This chapter will examine the habit of long-range vision casting coupled with constant monitoring processes to check and adjust the temperature for the culture you aim to create. We'll explore the integration of data use, the practice of zeroing in on your purpose as a leader as it pertains to leading the school's vision, the crucial need to foster hope for the community, and other leadership actions that not only streamline your efforts but amplify your impact. Don't forget to revisit and cultivate the habits developed in earlier chapters as you continue on your journey toward resilience!

CHAPTER 3

Be the Vision Caster

Melissa is a middle school principal with almost a decade of leadership experience at multiple schools. Grappling with the emotions of declining enthusiasm for her job, she sat down at the table with her leadership team in a summer planning meeting. She and the group were eager to begin the conversations about building upon their prior year's experiences and setting the stage for an impactful year ahead. As brainstorming began around where to establish priorities and determine a plan, she listened to each team member—several assistant principals, a director of teaching and learning, and a brand-new director of innovation. Ambitious ideas were brought forward that varied from a robotics program to a math intervention curriculum to supplement core courses, a grant application that would fund fine arts field trips, and many more. None were poor ideas, and many were likely to enrich students' lives, but Melissa stared down at the district administrator's agenda from a meeting the day before. As with the start of most school years, there was an array of information describing new and shifting expectations that the building leaders were expected to return and deliver with fidelity and no shortage of expediency. For example, she was about to tell her team that they also needed to prepare to implement a brand-new interim assessment system, as well as create a new Personal Finance course for seventh graders. She waited for a lull in the conversation and asked the group, "Team, I'm so happy to see how enthusiastic you are about all these great ideas. I need us to revisit a more important question before continuing: How do any of these programs bring us closer to delivering on our school's vision?" An uncomfortable silence settled in amongst the group as they pondered the idea, and Melissa knew now she needed to revisit the question herself.

WHY DEVELOP THE
HABIT OF CASTING A VISION

Education is a field overflowing with programs, materials, strategies, and resources that promise to *fix* whatever problem or challenge a school or teacher may face. Education leaders at all levels, while well-intended, are at risk for identifying a perceived need and leaping immediately to "solution-itis," a non-medical term for the habit of grasping for material responses to questions or challenges without first determining if the need for a new resource is appropriate. In some cases, this may be a result of scarce time to delve deeply into understanding systemic challenges. In others, a leader may lack experience to guide sustainable change but nonetheless be guided by an innate desire to help mitigate struggle faced by overwhelmed teachers. They may be at risk for compiling a broad collection of programs and materials touted as *turnkey* by vendors yet finding their school mired in *initiative overload* without a clear understanding of how to proceed. Researchers Fullan and Quinn characterize this approach as destructive and ineffective, naming *ad hoc policies* as the fourth *wrong driver* that works against school systems endeavoring to achieve reform (Fullan & Quinn, 2015, p. 4). Pursuing coherence is the only antidote to the siloed, disconnected, and reactive practice of too many initiatives for schools and districts. For leaders of schools or entire school systems, coherence reflects the routines and practices used to guide stakeholders toward a collective vision.

> *Pursuing coherence is the only antidote to the siloed, disconnected, and reactive practice of too many initiatives for schools and districts.*

A vision is contextualized, personalized, and internalized by an entire community. When a vision is not present, systems (and the communities that comprise them) are at risk of wandering into any and every direction that randomly appears as an option. As Melissa set the stage with her team for a new year, individuals dreamt up shiny new ideas or brought out personal passions rooted in their areas of specialty (technology, for example) as a potpourri of activities that might have an impact or might be a waste of time and money. Without an established vision, the coherence and purpose of any initiative—research-based or otherwise—is at risk for existing in a silo. Engagement in such initiatives may only be embraced by a few while the greater community acts out of compliance. Worse still, educators passively resist and disengage, touting the adage, "This too shall pass," as they have experienced the routine before and have yet to find it of value. A vision is a collaboratively developed outcome of coherent practices and processes that provides an important driver—the collective focus around a common purpose—for engaging stakeholders in change. Your engagement as a leader in specific practices, such as identifying your purpose, connecting your purpose to your daily work, and examining the values of your community, will predicate the successful and meaningful development of a vision for your community.

Routinely applying the habit of casting a vision will foster resilience in yourself and your school or district. For example, a sense of purpose (a foundational component of a strong vision) is described in research as contributing significantly to the individual's ability to experience resilience (Kim et al., 2014). Chapter 1 defines resilience as "the process and outcome of successfully adapting to difficult or challenging life experiences" (APA, n.d.). For school leaders, cultivating habits that foster resilience in themselves and others can be critical in navigating contemporary times of volatility, uncertainty, doubt, and constant change (VUCA) (Bennis & Nanus, 1985). Though often utilized to describe the mindsets and behaviors of individuals, organizational resilience is a characteristic of groups, businesses, or organizations, such as a school or district, that is also deeply connected to a sense of purpose held by both leaders and stakeholders (Lee & Dance, 2022; Nauck et al., 2021). Fullan and Quinn (2015) draw the connection between the moral purpose of the leader and the influence their purpose has on stakeholders: "Leaders must first understand their moral purpose and be able to combine personal values, persistence, emotional intelligence, and resilience. This is essential because their moral purpose will be reflected in all their decisions and actions" (p. 18). As leaders guide a community toward developing and pursuing an ambitious vision, a sense of purpose provides a sustaining and nourishing influence that the vision is worthy and meaningful. Consider these concepts against existing beliefs and understandings you may have held about casting a vision for your school or district (Figure 3.1).

FIGURE 3.1 ● Characteristics of Casting a Vision

CASTING A VISION IS . . .	CASTING A VISION IS NOT . . .
A collective endeavor involving the entire community	Accomplished solely by a single leader
An ongoing journey with many cycles of development	A process completed in a set period
Foundational to cultivating resilience throughout a community	Unrelated or disconnected from the overall health and well-being of the community
A process that invites all stakeholders to contribute toward the future of the school or district	Isolated to only the community's leaders as a way of documenting where they intend to lead the school or district

VISION CASTING BEGINS WITH YOUR "WHY"

Perhaps at some point in your educational journey or during your career, you have engaged in some form of an experience requiring you to identify a broader purpose for why you pursue the things that you pursue, interact with others in a certain way, or strive to have some form of impact on the world around you.

Pause and Reflect

Engage in an initial reflection on the experience you have had with exploring your purpose thus far.

What were the conditions under which you were inspired to examine your purpose (age, setting, reason, career phase, etc.)?

_____

_____

_____

_____

_____

If you arrived at a particular idea of your purpose, why do you believe you landed on that specific idea?

_____

_____

_____

_____

_____

Has purpose beneficially served you at any point in your life? Why or why not?

_____

_____

_____

_____

_____

_____

If you identified a purpose earlier in life, does that purpose still pertain to you today? Why or why not?

_____

_____

_____

_____

What external influences may cause you to adjust your purpose, given the opportunity (life changes, career shifts, etc.)?

_____

_____

_____

_____

Determining your purpose as a leader may reflect experiences you have had in your development over your career or may sound akin to a question that employers ask when interviewing you for an important role. Be cautious to dismiss this important and personal process as being trivial or perhaps something you're obligated to do by others. Finding meaning in your work is predicated on understanding why you engage in some behaviors and not others while leading your community or how you arrive at various decisions throughout the school day and year. If you have not previously invested time and effort into identifying your purpose, use the reflection questions here:

(Continued)

(Continued)

REFLECTION PROMPT	NOTES
Describe an *ideal state* of the future in which you characterize the adult versions of the students currently enrolled in your community (ways of thinking, civic engagement, accomplishments, interactions with others, impact on society, mindsets, etc.).	
How would you describe the most significant challenges and/or flaws in the global education system as they affect its stakeholders (students, families, staff)?	
When do you find yourself in *flow*—energized, intrinsically motivated, and driven—at work? Who is present? What are you working on? How did you arrive in this scenario?	
If you found yourself closing the door to your office for the last time tomorrow, what would you hope to be able to say you accomplished in your career?	

By analyzing the responses you generate to these reflection questions, you may see trends or patterns that suggest or clarify your beliefs about the purpose that your leadership serves. As you continue examining the habit of casting a vision and, in later chapters, connect your learning to other habits, such as managing change, be sure to revisit these responses and continue developing your ideas!

CONNECTING STAKEHOLDERS WITH YOUR "WHY"

Fullan and Quinn (2015) write, "Great leaders connect others to the reasons they became educators—their moral purpose" (p. 19). By examining and identifying your purpose, you will find opportunities to invite those around you to connect with and become inspired by the impact you aspire to make—your "why." As the leader of your community (department, school, district, network, etc.), you serve a variety of stakeholder groups in different ways. Determining the connection between your "why" and your relationship with them presents a unique opportunity to strengthen your impact. Figure 3.2 provides examples of how your leadership purpose may positively impact different stakeholder groups. Use the remaining spaces in the table to brainstorm ideas directly related to your purpose.

FIGURE 3.2 ● Leader Purpose and Your Impact on Stakeholder Groups

STAKEHOLDER GROUP (ACTUAL OR HYPOTHETICAL)	HOW YOUR PURPOSE MAY POSITIVELY IMPACT THIS GROUP
School board or other governing entity	**Possibilities:** Invite board members to tour your campus and meet members of your community as an opportunity to build positive relationships. **Your Ideas:**
District leaders	**Possibilities:** Galvanize community members from your school around district efforts to close achievement gaps for emergent bilingual learners. Initiate a new task force or committee to address declining attendance rates in district schools. **Your Ideas:**

(Continued)

(Continued)

STAKEHOLDER GROUP (ACTUAL OR HYPOTHETICAL)	HOW YOUR PURPOSE MAY POSITIVELY IMPACT THIS GROUP
School leaders	**Possibilities:** Lead a district committee as a liaison to the superintendent to voice issues of concern and advocate for fair working conditions. **Your Ideas:**
Systemwide job-alike colleagues (i.e., those in your same role within the same system)	**Possibilities:** Generate involvement amongst experienced leaders to engage as mentors for brand new or aspiring administrators. **Your Ideas:**
Classroom teachers and instructional staff	**Possibilities:** Advocate on behalf of instructional staff to compensate their time required to learn a new districtwide curriculum. **Your Ideas:**
Families/Parents/Guardians	**Possibilities:** Conduct empathy interviews with as many families as possible to understand the most effective ways to engage their involvement in the school community. **Your Ideas:**
Students	**Possibilities:** Initiate a new Career and Tech Education program available to any interested student. **Your Ideas:**

Upon finishing this reflection activity, return and revisit these ideas often! Routinely analyze the alignment between the actions you describe upon first completion, those you encounter as opportunities to engage or avoid, and the desired impact you aspire to have on others as a result of your leadership.

CONNECTING PURPOSE, VALUES, AND VISION

Following your experiences with personal reflection around your purpose as it guides your work as a leader, you are equipped to build upon your purpose toward a meaningful vision for the community of your school or system. Examining the visible and hidden values of the community presents an informative first step toward determining if there is coherence between the vision being developed (or already documented) and the beliefs, hopes, and aspirations of the individuals aspiring toward that vision. These values will articulate how individuals interact with each other on a daily basis while living out or embodying the vision. Inviting stakeholders to voice their opinions in the analysis of values will provide a critical perspective that guides your leadership efforts and engages those community members in the system's future.

Inviting stakeholders to voice their opinions in the analysis of values will provide a critical perspective that guides your leadership efforts and engages those community members in the system's future.

Before beginning the work, gather an inventory of data that may inform your next steps. Figure 3.3 shares some examples.

FIGURE 3.3 ● Understanding the Present State: A Data Inventory Chart

WHERE TO GATHER DATA	EXAMPLES OF HOW TO GATHER THE DATA	WHAT WILL THIS DATA INFORM?
Campus facilities (classrooms, common areas, etc.)	Conduct a thorough campus *artifact walk* of all areas, preferably when no one is on campus. Document what you see on the walls, the physical classroom resources, the *décor* of the various areas (trophy cases, for example, or other artifacts that convey the values of the community).	The design, décor, and structure of the campus's physical spaces convey significant messages about what the community values and prioritizes. Though the mission statement may include words such as innovation, the classrooms may not have any technology for teachers or students. You may notice student artwork on display that represents learning about diverse cultures, and this aligns with a school's value of embracing diversity.
From the school staff (all roles)	Conduct a *listening tour* and host individual or small group conversations with as many school staff members as possible. Ensure that every possible role is represented in the process, from bus drivers to teachers and everyone in between. While seeking volunteers can be authentic, review who volunteers and consider direct invitations to those not signing up. This ensures the representation of voices and ideas from the broadest range of individuals.	This 360-degree perspective of the school community members is likely to provide robust information! Depending upon your goal for this process, your questions may elicit ideas around how stakeholders feel they are valued and included in the school community. Another approach may lead you to examine if all stakeholders have equivalent beliefs about the effectiveness of the educational program offered at the school. With such a range of participants, you are bound to gain a very thorough understanding of your answers!
Local community members	Gather a selection of local community members to host conversations with. Ensure a diverse range of participants, for example: Leaders or owners of nearby businesses who are actively involved in the school and who are not at all involved in the school Real estate company representatives who have an interest in how the local schools inform their business Community leaders who are engaged in local policymaking, such as Councils, advocacy groups, or nonprofits, or other entities with an interest in the development of local youth	Data from these inquiries might inform whether the internal perception of the school's quality is in correspondence with the external community and present opportunities to enhance your efforts at nurturing a healthy reputation with potential and current families. Building confidence and a source of pride in the school by area community members may multiply the outcomes of your efforts to build confidence with existing families and be self-generative in positive outcomes!

WHERE TO GATHER DATA	EXAMPLES OF HOW TO GATHER THE DATA	WHAT WILL THIS DATA INFORM?
From school families (students included)	Identify a selection of families to host conversations with. It may not be at all possible to meet with all of them! Rather, develop your list to ensure the utmost diversity of perspective. For example: Families new to the school and those who have been there for many years (or with multiple children over time) Families of highly successful students and those who could be characterized as "struggling" Families of varying socioeconomic and cultural backgrounds Families who are very involved in the school and those who hardly ever come to campus Families who have unenrolled children in your school for any reason	This opportunity presents data that ensures you are not experiencing the effect of "blinders" or unconscious bias on how you perceive the effectiveness of any of the school's priorities. When a dominant population is benefiting from a program such as Advanced Placement courses, for example, it's easy to assume that all are benefiting when in fact it may be harming other groups. Students not tracked to engage in the courses may have very limited other options, an inequitable outcome that might be revealed by this data set.

Beginning with this thorough exploration of your community members' values, perceptions, mindsets, beliefs, and opinions will assist you in generating a deep understanding of the alignment between what becomes stated as the school's vision and how its stakeholders fully and authentically experience that vision. Later, in Chapter 7, you will have additional opportunities to examine even more ways to apply the data described here toward developing the vision. As you begin your journey toward developing and nurturing that vision, you will eventually engage many of these individuals alongside you in the building process.

ENGAGING THE COMMUNITY IN CASTING THE VISION

With a deeper foundational understanding of your own purpose as an educator and the broader community's values, the next steps toward determining a new vision for the future may begin. Just as in the initial process, you engaged a wide range of stakeholders; it's of utmost importance to continue doing so as you guide the process forward. Like the classroom teacher who co-creates the learning experience with their students, inviting the perspectives and ideas of those involved in the school elicits their sense of agency and ownership of the future of their community. Further, when community members feel they are seen, valued, and heard, they are likely to experience their own sense of psychological safety within the system, a factor contributing to their own resilience and the collective resilience of the group. Consider the following opportunities to involve stakeholders in the pursuit of a common vision:

SHARE, ANALYZE, AND SYNTHESIZE THE INVENTORY OF THE COMMUNITY'S VALUES

Beginning with an inventory of the data collection process outlined here, seek opportunities to synthesize the results and share them with different stakeholder groups in various ways. Resist the inclination to derive or assert that there are specific action steps or outcomes based on the inventory, at least when sharing with others. This will prevent your ideas from influencing how others receive and interpret the information. As stakeholders engage with the data, guide participants toward narrowing the information into trends or patterns that encompass broader themes. Whether you name them as shared agreements, value statements, community beliefs, philosophies, or other descriptors, ensure the utilization of consensus-building tools or strategies to elicit agreement across as many groups as possible as to those that become publicly and permanently shared.

CREATE A LEARNER PROFILE BASED ON THESE VALUES

In the process of casting a vision with your community, an effective approach can begin by developing a clear and common understanding of what you aspire to observe as the effect of your efforts on the learners in your system. For example, this may be called a "learner profile" or "profile of a graduate." Building upon the values analysis previously described, gather a comprehensive range of input into the characteristics of a learner in your system. You may determine this learner has completed all grades or levels in your setting. Others may specify that their learner profile reflects those currently enrolled in the school or differentiate characteristics as learners move through system divisions (elementary versus high school, for example). Regardless, begin with gathering a diverse and vast collection of ideas and continue by comparing these ideas to the values inventory for alignment or to prompt shifts in conversation. Once compiled, ensure consistent and ongoing communication of the learner profile across the entire community.

DOCUMENT THE IDEAL JOURNEY OF A STUDENT THROUGH YOUR SYSTEM

Another opportunity for examining community perspectives to ensure through-system alignment between what is stated as the vision, how stakeholders experience the system daily, and the outcomes of a learner's experience in the system is to ask the students! As an extension of the data-gathering process described, this approach entails strictly gathering information from the students or learners. Consider the need for confidentiality as a premise for the work and ensure all types of learners are represented when gathering data. Collect qualitative reports from the selected students and utilize them to create a narrative describing a student's journey through your system. Compare the student's experiences to the values inventory results and the learner profile for yet another triangulation opportunity as you seek to affirm that the school or district's vision is a deeply accurate reflection of the daily reality within the system.

We've established that galvanizing a community around a common vision is a powerful process fostering organizational resilience. With a collectively defined understanding of why the school exists and the intentions it serves, all involved are guided by a clear sense of direction. This may serve as the antidote to the *solution-itis* portrayed in the example of Melissa's leadership team at the start of the chapter. Grounded in its purpose, the community is more likely to experience resilience in the face of uncertainty, unforeseen disruption, obstacles, or change—a prerequisite for a successful journey toward a new future. Leading the community on this journey will also require highly effective collaboration across all stakeholders, and conditions must be nurtured for this to occur. Fullan and Quinn (2015) call "cultivating collaborative cultures" the third of four high-impact drivers that result in systemic reform, such as a comprehensive shift toward a new, collective vision. Collaboration, however, may be portrayed as physically bringing people together around a particular topic.

Grounded in its purpose, the community is more likely to experience resilience in the face of uncertainty, unforeseen disruption, obstacles, or change—a prerequisite for a successful journey toward a new future.

Pause and Reflect

When have I engaged my stakeholders in exploring and developing a vision?

_____

_____

_____

_____

_____

Who was involved in these experiences? Who was not involved?

_____

_____

_____

_____

_____

How would you describe the distinct experiences in which you engaged your stakeholders in exploring and developing a vision?

_____

_____

_____

_____

_____

What were the outcomes of these experiences?

_____

_____

_____

_____

_____

What changes in your leadership occurred because of these outcomes?

_____

_____

_____

_____

_____

What do you envision doing next as a result of comparing your previous efforts to the ideas in this chapter?

_____

_____

_____

_____

_____

VISION CASTING IS A JOURNEY, NOT A DESTINATION

In Chapter 10, you will learn about managing change by practicing mindsets and approaches that foster communities of risk-takers who work together in an environment characterized by psychological safety. In examining another habit, leading as a learner (Chapter 5), you will have opportunities to build upon the values and vision-casting strategies within this chapter to amplify the coherence for yourself and your community. The intent of foreshadowing these intersections is to highlight the experience and intent of vision-casting as an ongoing, iterative journey for all involved. The vision itself is not an objective to be achieved, but an ideal state that provides an ambitious and clear focus and necessitates the conditions for you and your stakeholders to work in unison. "This consistent, collective shaping and reshaping of ideas and solutions forges deep coherence across the system" (Fullan & Quinn, 2015, p. 47). Consider the Let's Reflect questions in this chapter and notice where your community is currently situated along the journey toward developing a vision.

The Big Ideas

In this chapter, you examined the connection between a sense of purpose for individuals and organizations and its influence on building resilience even in the face of challenging circumstances. Determining your own moral purpose as a leader in education is a fundamental first step toward guiding your community to do the same. Your ability to successfully cast an ambitious vision for every stakeholder will be driven by your own understanding of and confidence in the purpose you serve in the daily decisions you make and actions you take. After that, engaging staff, families, and students in a journey of determining a collective vision and articulating how each individual plays a role in striving toward it will comprise the substantive focus of your work as a leader. You are not only the vision caster but also the vision caretaker.

As the caretaker of the vision, employing the practices you examined in this chapter to determine your moral purpose as a leader, collaboratively identifying the community's values as a guidepost to shape the vision, and engaging stakeholders in building the vision will nurture and sustain the focus for all. Remaining curious and introspective will also enable you to continuously learn and adapt, and the next chapter frames a way of thinking and acting to foster this approach.

Let's Reflect

1. Building from your existing experience and knowledge, which of the strategies described in this chapter might impact your efforts to be both a vision caster and a vision caretaker for your community? Why do you feel that is true?

   _____

   _____

   _____

2. Before reading this chapter, what practices, strategies, resources, and ideas have you employed to develop a vision for your community and/or lead your community toward that vision? What impacted your outcomes most, and why do you believe that outcome was achieved?

   _____

   _____

   _____

3. What challenges do you face around cultivating organizational resilience in your setting? How will you endeavor to address those challenges?

_____

_____

_____

What's Next?

In Chapter 4, you will turn the magnifying lens on your mindsets, beliefs, behaviors, and attitudes as you develop the habit of _checking your blind spots_. In your efforts to thrive as a leader amidst any environment or scenario in which you find yourself, unpacking the assumptions (the _blind spots_) you hold about both yourself and others around you presents an opportunity to adjust and adapt in pursuit of continuous growth. Coupled with consistently applying the routines and practices learned about building boundaries and pouring them into your bucket first, you are well-prepared for tackling the forthcoming habits, such as managing change to sustain your well-being throughout your career!

CHAPTER 4

Check Your Blind Spots

Diego, a brand-new middle school principal beginning his role after eight years as the school's assistant principal, walked into the staff meeting equipped with a presentation he had spent hours creating. He was eager to tell the teachers about the upcoming initiative wherein they would all participate in a yearlong diversity, equity, inclusion, and justice (DEIJ) training with a consultant. As soon as his predecessor retired, Diego knew he could lead the school past its pervasive complacency around the concerning reports from students and families that the school culture was divisive and excessively focused on only pursuing ideas that benefited the dominant culture of high socioeconomic status, Caucasian families. Sharing his presentation, he was keenly aware of the skeptical expressions on teachers' faces, the whispers just out of his earshot during the coffee breaks, and the silence when he invited a debrief conversation at the end. Several months later, he had logged numerous phone calls from the teacher union reporting complaints of unfair mandates to participate in training and meetings "unrelated to instructional practice." While a fraction of the teaching staff eagerly tried the new approaches shared by the consultant, the vast majority refused even to attempt. The superintendent called him one afternoon by surprise. "Is this the hill you want to die on, Diego? I know you are a capable leader, but you might reconsider whether this is worth the fight." Diego was stunned. He had spent years listening to the reports from students and parents of underrepresented communities that they felt isolated, unappreciated, and even threatened at the school. He had been evident in his application for the job that changing this culture was one of his top priorities, and he never imagined the district would hire him if they did not align with his ideas. However, without any support from his superiors or, least of all, from the staff he now led, he suddenly worried that his first principalship might also be his last.

WHY FOCUS ON THE HABIT OF CHECKING YOUR BLIND SPOTS

When leaders encounter opposition, challenges, or setbacks, it is not unusual to wonder, "How did I not see that coming?" We characterize these unanticipated experiences as "blind spots." However, learning to recognize and understand potential reactions, obstacles, or other types of scenarios that may occur because of leadership decisions is a habit that can be developed with routine practices around identifying and regularly pausing to check blind spots. As you develop the habit of casting a vision for your community, for example, you may experience increased excitement and zeal for the future you strive for. Amidst your enthusiasm and positive mindset, you may need to anticipate the stakeholders might engage in the process out of a sense of compliance rather than commitment. If you had checked your blind spot and anticipated this resistance, you could have slowed down the implementation timeline to create more opportunity for buy-in. There is no perfect recipe for becoming aware of every possible blind spot a leader may encounter. However, research points to patterns of human behavior that enable you to understand those significant areas likely to influence your leadership effectiveness.

> There is no perfect recipe for becoming aware of every possible blind spot a leader may encounter. However, research points to patterns of human behavior that enable you to understand those significant areas likely to influence your leadership effectiveness.

In the daily work of education leadership, becoming consumed by the rapid pace and cognitively demanding aspects of the job can be common. You may desire the time to pause and reflect on previous experiences to inform continuous improvement, as well as the bandwidth to anticipate and analyze the potential outcomes of initiatives you may implement. Instead, the flow of information and expectations placed upon you may often feel as though it only arrives precisely when they need to be addressed. Operating at this high speed on a regular basis is likely to cause you to experience a constant state of overwhelm and increase the risk that you will miss cues and other details crucial to your success. External cues may show up as behavioral reactions from stakeholders, mistakes that negatively influence the progress of a project, or resistant attitudes by group members, for example. While you may or may not always be sensitive to the presence of these cues, learning to recognize them and anticipate them in the context of different circumstances is fundamental to checking your blind spots. Throughout this chapter,

FIGURE 4.1 ● Characteristics of Blind Spots

CHECKING YOUR BLIND SPOTS IS	CHECKING YOUR BLIND SPOTS IS NOT
Intentionally making time to understand behavior patterns, beliefs, and biases in yourself and others	Never pausing to consider how your actions influence the personal experiences of your stakeholders
Noticing how different stakeholder groups react to your leadership practices and determining how your behaviors and communication may merit adjustment to achieve a goal	Learning that you may have specific blind spots (behaviors, biases, or beliefs) and continuing to act or communicate as you have always done in the past
Internalizing the belief that, as a leader, you have a responsibility to make shifts in your practice to ensure the well-being and success of all stakeholders	Believing that others should accept you for who you are and that it is the responsibility of stakeholders to adapt to your leadership
Recognizing that blind spots can also be areas that negatively affect your well-being, not only the well-being of others	Assuming that blind spots pertain only to how your actions affect others and believing you are impervious to being personally affected

you will have an opportunity to develop your understanding of distinct beliefs held by you and those around you, biases that influence your interactions with stakeholders and that can inform shifts in your practice, and behaviors you may unknowingly demonstrate that correlate to typical reactions and interactions affecting your leadership practice. As you embark on an exploration of common blind spots for education leaders, notice the distinctions between what does and does not characterize the habit of checking for blind spots (Figure 4.1).

BUILDING YOUR BLIND SPOT IQ

Blind spots are unique to each individual leader and are based on personal background, experience, and circumstance. However, examining common types of blind spots enables you to consider those for which you may be more at risk, as well as others that do not pertain to your current environment. Consider each of the various beliefs, behaviors, and biases that follow as you develop your understanding of common blind spots. Utilize the reflection guides throughout to examine your leadership practice for areas of further development and growth.

Examining common types of blind spots enables you to consider those for which you may be more at risk, as well as others that do not pertain to your current environment.

BELIEFS AS BLIND SPOTS

Beliefs about almost any topic—what constitutes effective leadership or how to build quality relationships with stakeholders, for example—can serve as a superpower or become their form of blind spot. While you may possess ample evidence from prior experience that your beliefs serve you well and benefit those around you, this evidence can prevent you from becoming aware of anomalies or opposing perspectives held by others. The failure to notice or recognize evidence that contradicts your beliefs is a specific pathway toward experiencing the negative effect of a blind spot. In Figure 4.2, explore the different but common beliefs in education leadership. As you notice the examples of each belief, compare your experience and identify how this belief either has influenced your leadership or might influence your leadership in the future.

FIGURE 4.2 ● Examples of Beliefs as Blind Spots

INFALLIBILITY
Leaders who believe they are responsible for the success and well-being of all their stakeholders may simultaneously believe they are capable of superhuman exertion. By consistently placing the needs of others before their own, the physical and mental demands of their daily work will unquestionably deplete even the most capable leaders' ability to be successful.

Real-Life Scenario:	**Responsive Practice to Prevent Blind Spots:**
The leader who holds a belief of infallibility will fill their schedule with an overwhelming majority of time spent with others meeting their needs and find themselves doing their own work late into the night and on the weekends. This sacrifices their rest and personal time. They will feel a sense of pride for never using sick leave or individual days, and yet their health will always be a last priority.	As a first step toward mitigating the effects of believing you are infallible, reexamine the strategies described in Chapter 1 on setting boundaries. Examine your personal beliefs that lead you to overexert yourself to the point of self-harm—you may work in a culture of *toxic productivity* that urges you to behave this way, for example. Celebrate your personal growth as you implement boundaries and replace your sense of reward for unhealthy exertion with rewards for applying limits to your level of self-sacrifice.

UNCONSCIOUS INCOMPETENCE
Understandably, leaders at any level may assume by having achieved the position title that they inherently possess sufficient knowledge and experience to accomplish the work. Encountering experiences in which you do not have adequate expertise, however, can present discomfort and avoidance. Further, recognizing the scenarios for which you are unprepared or require support may present a blind spot wherein you are unaware of what you do not yet know.

Real-Life Scenario:	**Responsive Practice to Prevent Blind Spots:**
When desiring to convey expertise and competence, a leader may assert their knowledge of a topic or area of work they know little or nothing about. Leaders who are unconsciously incompetent resist feedback and	Reflect on past experiences when you were a beginner at something (a hobby, a job, etc.) and notice the positive emotions from those memories—excitement at small accomplishments, for example. Approach a new

UNCONSCIOUS INCOMPETENCE

avoid opportunities for external support such as coaching or mentoring. They may experience dissonance with teachers in an evaluative setting as they strive to convey their expertise in areas where the teachers know much more.

challenge to embrace the beginner's mindset and enjoy the novelty and rapid growth. Identify a scenario in which you would feel comfortable gathering feedback from others on your decisions. Seek out several individuals for this feedback and commit to applying it immediately, then reward yourself in some way for your risk-taking!

UNMANAGEABLE STRESS

While stress is unavoidable in any profession, resting in the belief that stress cannot be appropriately and effectively managed is a sure path toward burnout. You learned explicit strategies to address this belief as you examined the habits of building boundaries and filling your bucket. Just as leaders have a responsibility to support the well-being of stakeholders, you also have a responsibility to learn and apply these skills to be most effective as a leader.

Real-Life Scenario:

Believing that stress is a regular aspect of the job is reflected in leaders who actively resist sources of support for stress management (e.g., coaching, counseling, or physical activity) to the point of self-harm. These leaders may develop elevated anxiety and irritability, becoming ineffective at navigating healthy relationships with stakeholders as a result. The stress can become so normalized that it becomes habit-forming, and a leader may seek to maintain high pressure and intensity.

Responsive Practice to Prevent Blind Spots:

As an initial step toward learning to manage stress, examine the strategies and practices described in Chapter 2. Take time to document the primary sources of your stress: individuals, tasks, time management, etc. For the noticeable contributors, explore new learning to improve your work habits. Is the source mainly the lack of time to do things? Investigate tools for organizing schedules and practice boundary-setting skills from Chapter 1. Is it particular tasks? Commit to a goal of improving your delegation and prioritization practices.

IMPLICIT STAKEHOLDER TRUST

Believing that your stakeholders' trust is implicit: In a leadership position, you may think stakeholders should inherently trust you because of your position in your school or district. Assuming the presence of trust, however, may disguise your understanding of stakeholders' need to be continuously engaged, informed, and supported during change experiences.

Real-Life Scenario:

A leader who believes that others must trust them inherently may independently decide to initiate a new program for the school and be surprised when stakeholders resist involvement or do not show enthusiasm. They may rarely provide context or explanation about changes in general, routinely expecting that the community simply believes the purpose and goals must be worthy.

Responsive Practice to Prevent Blind Spots:

With the exception of instances where you have longstanding relationships with stakeholders, trust is rarely implicit. Embracing this fact is an initial step to developing the mindset that you must perpetually strive to earn and sustain the trust others have in you. Explore the blind spot of communication, for example, as a strategy for aligning your words and behaviors to cultivate trust in your community. Consistently seek feedback from stakeholders to demonstrate your interest in their input and also ensure you act intentionally in response. Seeing you change due to the input will enhance stakeholders' trust when you convey that you care about their needs.

Pause and Reflect

Among the beliefs described in Figure 4.2 that are familiar sources of blind spots for leaders, what might be most likely to influence your effectiveness as a leader?

_____

_____

_____

_____

_____

BEHAVIORS AS BLIND SPOTS

While beliefs can influence how we take care of ourselves or inform how we interact with others, our behaviors consist of the actions we take or do not take as we engage with the different stakeholders in our community. Nonverbal behaviors have a tremendous capacity for communicating what we feel and think to others, sometimes even more clearly than words. Often, our behavior represents our inner thoughts and preferences. As a leader, when your words and actions do not align, your stakeholders will likely experience confusion or distrust. Consider the examples in Figure 4.3 of different categories of behavior commonly demonstrated by those who lead others. As you read, notice the potential connection between the described behaviors and the beliefs you read about in the prior section.

FIGURE 4.3 ● Examples of Behaviors as Blind Spots

MARTYR BEHAVIOR	
The tendency to perceive that you possess characteristics, knowledge, and experience that equips you to feel often responsible for *fixing* others' problems and challenges whether or not they are interested or need your support. Martyrs gain increased feelings of self-worth for caring for others they perceive as struggling or adversely challenged.	
Real-Life Scenario:	**Responsive Practice to Prevent Blind Spots:**
Leaders who demonstrate martyr behavior (also known as savior complex or messiah complex) may always be the last to leave campus and are sure that the community knows how busy, needed, and noble they are for doing so. They may be at risk for *coddling* staff or students and avoid upholding high expectations to protect their role as caregivers/providers.	Martyr's behavior may be effectively addressed by improving skills in setting boundaries such as those described in Chapter 1. When interacting with others, articulate that you are making a personal choice to exert extra time or effort but that does not come with an expectation that they do the same. Practice removing yourself from situations where you are inclined to step in and resolve others' problems or mistakes.

FRIENDING THE TEAM	
Leaders who experience an elevated desire to be liked, valued, or appreciated by others may also demonstrate the behavior of befriending those whom they supervise to earn this appreciation. This may result in an adverse effect of becoming at risk for affording preferential treatment to stakeholders in return for friendship or allowing behaviors otherwise not aligned with established expectations.	
Real-Life Scenario:	**Responsive Practice to Prevent Blind Spots:**
When an expectation is set, for example, that everyone attends the professional development workshop and several staff choose not to without reason, this type of leader may overlook the needed admonitions and recourse so as not to cause conflict or dissonance. A leader who is friends with some staff more than others is at risk of being seen as unfair and untrustworthy by those who do not seek a more positive relationship with their supervisor.	Consider what your stakeholders need from your leadership to boost their engagement: support, direction, concern for their well-being, clear purpose, etc. Accept responsibility for your actions when you notice you respond differently to different individuals, and seek consistency across all groups. Develop your superpowers in having difficult conversations that preserve healthy relationships and support holding your entire community to a standard of high expectation.

COMPLACENCY	
When a leader experiences a sense of confidence and comfort from holding a high level of authority or power, complacent behavior may show up as a diminished effort toward upholding high expectations or fulfilling obligations. Further, "people may overvalue your ideas and undervalue theirs" (Diamond et al., 2024, para. 1).	
Real-Life Scenario:	**Responsive Practice to Prevent Blind Spots:**
Complacent leaders may choose not to attend meetings, workshops, or events with their stakeholders when, in fact, their presence conveys a level of importance to the activity. Excessive task delegation is another symptom of complacency, particularly in avoidance of difficult conversations with parents or staff members, for example.	Collaborate with middle-level leaders to equally distribute all types of tasks, and you will not only keep a better pulse on the school culture, you will model to your team that you are fully engaged in the work you ask them to do. For example, you might also find new opportunities to engage with staff in their daily work, such as substitute for a class, volunteer for a fundraiser, or answer the office phone for an hour each day.

(Continued)

COMMUNICATION
While communication is not in itself a blind spot, recognizing the many ways in which communication influences leadership practices is crucial to developing the habit of checking one's blind spots.

Real-Life Scenario:	**Responsive Practice to Prevent Blind Spots:**
At the start of the year, leaders share immense expectations for staff to comply with mundane tasks such as entering attendance, signing up for extra duties, and more. Resentment can build when requirements are not met, premised on the assumption of being ignored when, in fact, the expectation was simply forgotten. In another example, the absence of adequate communication about the purpose of a new initiative presents significant risks for stakeholders to experience confusion, resistance, or uncertainty.	When sharing information, create a simple filtering system to assist recipients in efficiently placing details within their priorities. For example, use email subject lines with action phrases, such as "For Awareness Only," "Action Required," or "Coming Up Next." Share information in multiple ways at multiple times, viewing interactions with others as a sequence of events: the before, the in-the-moment, and the follow-up. The maximum effect of both these strategies is to utilize a common location for storing different categories of information.

Pause and Reflect

As you learned about the different types of behavior that can lead to blind spots in your leadership, what did you notice about the connection between the behaviors and the beliefs described in the prior section?

_____

_____

_____

_____

_____

BIASES AS BLIND SPOTS

Biases are mental shortcuts that we all use, and unconscious or implicit biases can guide our behaviors without us being aware of their impact. As Banaji and Greenwald (2016) explain in *Blindspot: Hidden Biases of Good People*, "the signal property of the mind does a great deal of its work automatically, unconsciously, and unintentionally" (p. 68), and they stress that this is "ordinary mental functioning." To be human is to have biases. However, those in supervisory positions must examine their unconscious biases and consider methods for mitigating their impact. While many types of bias exist, we will examine a few that are especially pervasive in education leadership and consider opportunities for responsive practice that enable you to mitigate their effect on those you lead (see Figure 4.4).

FIGURE 4.4 ● Examples of Biases as Blind Spots

AFFINITY BIAS
The tendency to be influenced by personal preferences for specific practices or behaviors like our own and those we perceive as favorable. For example, Banaji and Greenwald (2016) note, "Economists, sociologists, and psychologists have repeatedly confirmed that the social group to which a person belongs can be isolated as a definitive cause of the treatment he or she receives" (p. 121). This does not just refer to adverse treatment but includes preferential treatment.

Real-Life Scenario:	Responsive Practice to Prevent Blind Spots:
Administrators who tend to work extra-long hours may be less positively oriented toward teachers with obligations that require them to leave work early occasionally. In other circumstances, a leader may be attracted to a teacher's disposition if it resembles characteristics that they value (optimism, for example, or similar energy levels) which may then lead them to believe the teacher is inherently a competent teacher. However, the two things are independent of each other.	One strategy to mitigate the effect of affinity bias is to share decision-making processes with others. As a team, you may be less likely to revert to always choosing a direction or response that benefits a certain group or individual. Affinity bias is extreme in interviewing processes. Develop and consistently apply a strong protocol involving unconscious bias training and inclusion of diverse perspectives throughout.

ATTRIBUTION BIAS
The inclination to make judgments about behaviors as though they were inherent personality traits. If someone is successful at something, leaders may downplay it as luck rather than actions, and failures may be linked to their personality rather than outside factors.

Real-Life Scenario:	Responsive Practice to Prevent Blind Spots:
Leaders from the dominant culture may attribute teacher performance, such as managing student behavior, as inherent to their character (e.g., disinterest in building connections with students) rather than situational context. On the other hand, they may attribute a teacher's ability to connect well with students to their young age, not recognizing that they have worked hard to develop communication, trust building, and listening skills geared toward adolescents.	Collecting qualitative and quantitative data about a scenario or individual serves to create a *bias buster* and more accurately inform your decisions and thoughts. For example, while your mind may jump to a conclusion based on attribution bias, take time to create data sources around the judgment: What exactly happened? Why might it have happened? What other patterns contradict your judgment? What might other perspectives reveal?

(Continued)

(Continued)

CONFIRMATION BIAS

The tendency to interpret information in a manner that confirms or supports preexisting beliefs about another person, even if the evidence is to the contrary. The horn or halo effect is a subset of confirmation bias.

Real-Life Scenario:	Responsive Practice to Prevent Blind Spots:
If an observer's first interaction with a teacher is negative, he may only focus on information that supports this belief during the observation, ignoring positive attributes. In addition, if a supervisor has a terrific first conversation with a new teacher, that teacher may benefit from the halo effect, where only positive attributes are focused on, and we are blind to the areas for improvement.	A simple way to mitigate the effect of confirmation bias is to seek out the ways in which you might be wrong rather than how you might be right. If this seems complicated (because you are so confident you are right!), seek the perspectives of others and ask them for opposing views. Alternatively, recall past experiences when your beliefs have been proven wrong and determine what changed your mind. Seek to reapproach the current scenario from this same lens.

CULTURAL BIAS

This stems from differences in cultural backgrounds between a leader and others around them (teachers, colleagues, families, etc.) that may manifest as language proficiency, accent, teaching styles, or cultural references. Cultural bias refers to the tendency to interpret and judge phenomena, actions, or people according to the standards of one's own culture.

Real-Life Scenario:	Responsive Practice to Prevent Blind Spots:
A leader may more favorably evaluate a teacher who uses instructional resources representative of their own culture, or another leader may perceive a teacher as less equipped for success because their accent is one with which they need to be more familiar. A leader may misinterpret the behaviors of parents as being disinterested and nonengaged when, instead, the school culture is not welcoming and inclusive.	Learn how to create and use an Empathy Map, a simple tool to guide new thinking about the experiences of those you supervise or with whom you interact. Focus on an individual or group and generate ideas around what they did, what they said, what they thought, and what they felt. Considering their perspectives in the latter two increases your propensity for understanding their choices and mindsets. Subsequently, you will be more likely to find entry points of understanding and relationship-building.

To be human is to have biases. However, those in supervisory positions must examine their unconscious biases and consider methods for mitigating their impact.

Pause and Reflect

Among the different types of bias listed in Figure 4.4, how might you believe they have previously influenced your leadership practice? What will you take as a first step toward minimizing the effect of your biases on your leadership?

_____

_____

_____

_____

_____

The Big Ideas

Chapter 4 has taken you further on the journey of introspection and self-reflection as you determined how unforeseen reactions, obstacles, and interpersonal dynamics may be more predictable and understood when you recognize where you have "blind spots" or areas of unconscious incompetence. By first learning to identify what blind spots are and where your background, culture, and experiences may influence those that you possess, you begin the process of knowing their presence. Taking this knowledge forward, the critical next steps of applying this learning to your work as a leader of the community's vision have displayed the notion that across every stakeholder, blind spots play a different role. By approaching every new initiative, project, question, or challenge with curiosity and flexibility, you are empowered to seek empathy for those you interact with and more deeply understand how to effectively engage them in the vision as a contributor, not a bystander.

Investing in personal reflection and growth has been the predominant focus of the early habits described in these chapters thus far. Knowing how to lead yourself may be seen as a prerequisite to leading others; therefore, the essential habits for initial focus have involved examining your scope of understanding about what you require (buckets) and what you must eliminate or reject (boundaries) to be of utmost service to your community. Now, expanding your purview to recognize those beliefs, mindsets, and attitudes (blind spots) you possess that influence your leadership has positioned your approach toward the challenges of leading the school or community toward its most ambitious vision.

Let's Reflect

1. How has bias (of any form) potentially influenced your relationships with others in your work? What ideas from this chapter might you apply to enhance your practice of *checking your blind spots* concerning bias?

_____

_____

_____

2. In what ways does your well-being influence your ability to be effective as a leader of others? What specific goals might you utilize to intentionally mitigate the adverse effects of stress and be the best version of yourself?

_____

_____

_____

3. How do you believe blind spots may affect your efforts toward casting a vision for your school or district's community? What ideas from this chapter will you apply the next time you endeavor to engage in leading the community toward its vision?

_____

_____

_____

What's Next?

Building upon the habit of *checking your blind spots* as you strive to both invest in your well-being (through boundaries and buckets) and cast an ambitious vision for your school or district, you are about to embark now on learning the habit of leading as a learner. With a strong foundation in caring for yourself and your community, you are ready to delve deeply into one of the most critical priorities of your work: guiding a compelling journey toward learning and growth. Equipped with an understanding of how blind spots can shape and influence your thinking and decision-making, it is time to leverage your skills and become a transformative, human-centered leader who guides others toward a vision of excellence for every learner!

CHAPTER 5

Habits of
Lead Learners

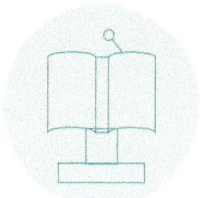

Eric, a veteran high school principal with fourteen years of experience, was planning an upcoming staff development day for his staff. Eric had just attended a district training where he came away from the experience complaining about the ineffective use of time allotted to learn about things he did not feel applied to his school community. He recognized that he needed to adjust his attitude as the lead learner of his own school. However, this top-down leadership professional development day helped Eric recognize the frustration his staff might feel as they sat in professional development. He found himself reflecting on a conversation with a mentor around some crucial differences between professional development and professional learning. He recognized that both had a purpose but that he wanted to provide professional learning opportunities as often as possible as a lead learner for his team. Eric wanted to create an environment as the lead learner where teachers could develop their learning goals and have a voice and choice in developing those strategies and goals over time. Eric also wanted to reflect on areas where he wanted to grow personally and areas of strength he could share with others. As the lead learner of his school, Eric saw these practices as integral to modeling a growth mindset where people could identify areas of relative strength and areas for improvement. Eyeing the school's vision on his office wall that described a community of learners, not solely students as learners, he knew he could be more intentional at delivering on that concept. His mentor often reminded him that if he truly aspired to cultivate young people who experienced a sense of ownership and agency around their learning, he would have to begin by developing this mindset in his teachers and himself. With the complexities of managerial tasks that often seemed to consumer his time, it seemed daunting, but necessary.

WHY INVEST IN THE HABIT OF BEING A LEAD LEARNER

The concept of "lead learner" is not novel, yet fully understanding its application to instructional leadership is an area of perpetual growth for most leaders. Whether implementing a new curriculum, guiding Multi-Tiered Systems of Support (MTSS) efforts, synthesizing student achievement data to inform critical decisions, or observing instruction to foster teacher professional growth, leaders are without question expected to know and understand an incredible amount of information. Furthermore, the phrase "lead learner" has become very popular, and you can find many blogs and articles about the topic. This concept applies both to the education field and the business field, which is another indicator that this specific habit is essential as we seek resilience. Recently, Hopkin wrote in a business journal, "Learning is one of the key tenets of leadership. Great leaders are learners. They read voraciously. They write and teach what they learn. Learning is as much a part of their life as eating. Learning is key to developing new ideas to improve your business and ensure success. Learning is the key to growth. Leaders who are learners 'raise the tide' for everyone around them." (Hopkin, 2016, p. 4). It is evident that remaining in the growth mindset and being actively involved in your goal setting and science of improvement cycles are important habits to model and engage in. However, using the phrase "lead learner" with your staff while not embracing or living out your learning could be seen as hypocrisy and could damage or *lower the tide* of the learning culture in your school. As Hopkins mentioned, lead learners can raise the tide; we might add that this is only true when done authentically. As lead learners, modeling the learning process while naming the powerful moves you are working through helps adult learners to engage in their science of learning cycles. Creating or maintaining a culture of learning is a common leadership priority. However, the challenge lies in modeling your learning for all the staff and students to observe. See Figure 5.1 for ideas on how you can model your learning for others.

FIGURE 5.1 ● Characteristics of Lead Learners

WHAT LEAD LEARNERS DO . . .	WHAT LEAD LEARNERS DO NOT DO . . .
Actively and collaboratively engage with educators	Lead from a podium and dump information onto or into the teachers and learners
Focus primarily on teacher learning and development	Focus primarily on building procedures and management
Connect their educators to differentiated resources and proactively seek professional learning opportunities for themselves and for their staff	Create professional development that is one size fits all for their educators
Take risks and embrace the science of improvement	Embrace perfectionism

*Remaining in the growth mindset and being actively involved
in your goal setting and science of improvement cycles
are important habits to model and engage in.*

LEADING THE LEARNING OF YOUR TEAM

Leaders are empowered to inspire significant impact for their team when they cultivate a thriving professional learning system for all. Yet in designing and leading learning for others, you may be at risk for implementing a *one-size-fits-all* approach in pursuit of efficiency, or perhaps selecting programs or trainings that appear meaningful at first but are disconnected from the ever-important vision of the school. In Chapter 3, we leaned into the habit of casting a clear vision for your community. Therefore, when focusing on the habit of being a lead learner, it is essential that you determine the "why" around the prioritization of continuous learning and frequently revisit your vision with your staff. There also needs to be clear through lines and connections between the professional learning opportunities chosen for teams/individuals that align back to the vision. Helping the team to focus or realign their engagement in professional learning to the vision that has been set will foster a common language and simplify planning and prioritizing for implementation.

As you endeavor to develop a comprehensive professional learning system, it is also crucial to be extremely mindful of initiative overload or the state experienced by individuals when leaders impose an extraordinary amount of new programs and practices at once without providing adequate time to implement. Begin proactively mitigating this experience by remembering that effective professional learning isn't about top-down mandates—it works best when teachers feel they have a voice and choice in the process. Make it clear that this is their program as much as it is the school's. As you strategically pursue utmost effective opportunities with teachers, not for them, prioritize deeper, more sustained engagement as part of an ongoing cycle over single events with no system for applying the learning. For example, an effective lead learner may create structures to offer follow-up coaching, peer observation opportunities, or learning communities that continue beyond initial workshops or training sessions.

How you show up as a participant in the professional learning experiences in the school offers a tremendous opportunity to model your leadership as a learner, too. When you participate as a learner, for example, in trainings or workshops, or engage in book studies, or collaborate in PLCs, as described in the next section, your presence signals that learning is a priority for everyone.

Should you engage in a learning experience of your own, too, you might model reflective behavior with your team by sharing how the experience shaped your leadership and helped you to grow in certain areas. This openness creates an authentic model of the vulnerability you are asking teachers to embrace and fosters growth and collaboration. In Chapter 8, you'll examine the habit of leveraging feedback as a lead learner. Incorporating feedback opportunities for teachers to provide input throughout the implementation of the professional learning system is an explicit example of this habit and how it mutually supports your habits of becoming a lead learner for your team.

When you participate as a learner, for example, in trainings or workshops, or engage in book studies, or collaborate in PLCs, as described in the next section, your presence signals that learning is a priority for everyone.

Attending to the alignment of all professional learning pursuits to the established vision of the school creates a model for your teachers and for your own growth that is driven by a clear purpose. Grounding all stakeholders' learning in a focus on "why" is likely to instill collective efficacy across the team as everyone is engaged in a collective pursuit of growth tied to a sense of direction. Thereafter, fending off *initiative overload* is a requisite practice to ensure your team has the full mental bandwidth to pursue meaningful experiences free from distraction. Embedding these approaches demonstrates to your team that learning for every member of the community is vital to the success of the students in your classrooms.

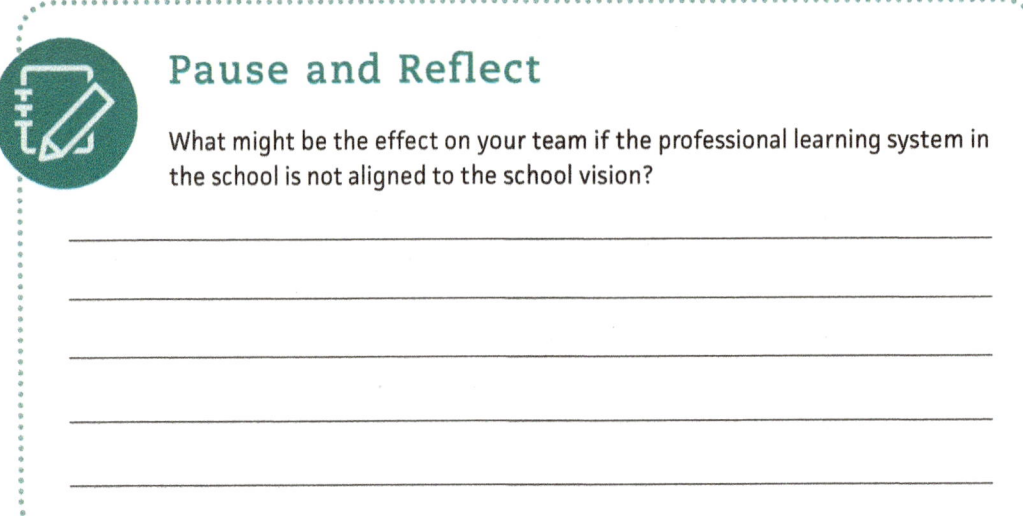

Pause and Reflect

What might be the effect on your team if the professional learning system in the school is not aligned to the school vision?

_____

_____

_____

_____

_____

LEADING THE LEARNING IN PROFESSIONAL LEARNING COMMUNITIES

Professional Learning Communities (PLCs) are another important avenue for leading the learning for adults in the school, yet they can be intimidating for leaders. At times, we find ourselves facilitating or observing content and/or pedagogy that is outside our area of expertise. The first thing to recognize as a lead learner of Professional Learning Communities is that you do not and cannot be the content specialist in every PLC. However, you can help to guide and facilitate collaborative learning among educators to improve teaching practices and student outcomes. As the lead learner, it is also important to make sure that all participants understand that they are not expected to know everything. The foundation of a PLC, according to Solution Tree, is, "It is not a meeting. It is a way of being!" PLCs are the way the adults in a school decide to act and work together to ensure high levels of learning for all students. They are a commitment to continuous improvement (Seif, 2024). As the lead learner, it is crucial that you continue to help guide the culture and mindset of the adults in the professional learning community. Establishing clear goals with the group, not for the group, helps educators to see you as a learner in the school community as well.

Pause and Reflect

Use the Establishing Goals chart to help you get started with what you want to achieve within each of your PLC teams:

Establishing Goals

HOW/WHAT CAN IMPACT STUDENT PERFORMANCE?	WHAT PROFESSIONAL LEARNING ENHANCEMENTS DO WE NEED TO DO THIS?	WHAT TEACHING STRATEGIES WILL CONTRIBUTE TO GROWTH AND ACHIEVEMENT FOR ALL STUDENTS?

As a lead learner in the PLC, it is essential to guide and contribute to a collaborative culture. As a leader, if you sit in the PLC and observe the team but do not contribute, this can impact the culture and productivity of the team as they perceive you may be there in an evaluative nature. It is important to begin by sharing the role you are playing within the PLC. Leaders may choose to observe PLCs for evaluation purposes at times. Initially, it is essential to let the PLC know whether you are in a collaborator mindset as the lead learner or an evaluative leader who will be providing specific feedback to the PLC team. Being clear about your intentions and purpose for participating will help to build trust so that the team will share creative ideas and be vulnerable with their challenges and successes. Thereafter, you must ensure you align your actions to your words so as to preserve the trust you are asking teachers to afford you. Engage in the collaborative experience from the stance of a collaborator. Prioritize asking questions as opposed to providing answers, for example. Use word choices that emphasize the collective approach such as "we" instead of "I" or "you all." Resist the urge to resolve challenging questions or topics with which participants are grappling (due to level of experience, for example) by listening and probing reflective thinking with question stems such as, "I wonder . . ." or "Given your knowledge of these students, what do you think . . . ?" If you are able to model uncertainty or areas where you are not an expert, you will invite participants to recognize the environment is safe to take such risks! Never behave inauthentically, but in the presence of opportunities to show you have room to learn like everyone else, consider sharing that with the PLC group. Embracing the behaviors of an effective learner will communicate to your team that you embody the words you articulate around serving as the lead learner of the community.

LEADING THE LEARNING THROUGH INSTRUCTIONAL FOCUS

As a lead learner, it is incumbent on you to provide the instructional staff in your school with the utmost opportunity to develop agency, grow as professionals, and experience success. This goal rests in your ability to nurture a collaborative culture of professionalism, transparency, and respect. Effective lead learners prioritize engaging actively in the continuous analysis and refinement of instructional excellence in every classroom. For example, as a lead learner who is responsible for instructional rounds, teacher evaluation, and the overall instructional effectiveness across the school, it is essential for you to embrace a mindset of curiosity and model an inquiry-driven approach during observations and debriefs. This is an area where aligning your actions to your words is of profound importance. Creating a foundation of trust amongst and between teachers and leaders requires intentional practices by a lead learner to instill confidence in teachers that they are empowered to take risks and be supported throughout their professional growth journey. The following are several approaches you may take as a lead learner to nurture this confidence and continuous improvement for teachers:

1. **Utilize Common Language Around Teaching and Learning:** A school staff may be comprised of educators with vastly diverse backgrounds and levels of experience. Regardless, establishing the foundation of a common language across every grade and subject that describes teaching practices, not teachers, is an essential early step to fostering transparency and ensuring validity of evaluations. Using the Danielson Framework for Teaching (Danielson et al., 2024), for example, provides a universal guide that encompasses the myriad domains of teaching from which clear, consistent observations may be conducted. By beginning with this in place, teachers may trust that they and their observer are working with a mutual understanding of what will be observed and/or evaluated.

2. **Acknowledge the Influence of Unconscious Bias on Instructional Observations:** Before engaging in fair, productive conversations with teachers about their teaching practices, leaders must recognize different types of bias and when they may be present in your efforts at examining instructional practice in classrooms. You explored the effect biases may have as a source of blind spots in your leadership in Chapter 4. Applying your understanding of the distinct types of biases presents an outstanding opportunity to model vulnerability and a willingness to continuously refine your own learning as a leader because you will be required to open your mind to being influenced by something out of your control. While unconscious bias cannot be cured, it can be addressed. By ensuring annual implicit bias training for anyone conducting observations, for example, you are able to bring the unconscious to the conscious level and heighten your awareness of your proclivities before formal observations occur. It may feel as though this is something that is hard to commit to because of time or money, but keep the focus on the impact it will have for your teachers and your community. Research has shown that repeated applications of modest interventions can provide a means for lessening some of our persistent stereotypes and associations.

Pause and Reflect

As you consider how unconscious bias may influence your impact as a lead learner, revisit the bias descriptions you examined in Chapter 4. Use this chart to help reflect on the four different biases and how that might be impacting instructional rounds, feedback cycles, and your overall school culture. If needed, use the descriptions in the following bias reflection matrix to help you reflect.

	HOW DO THESE BIASES POTENTIALLY SHOW UP PRIOR TO DOING INSTRUCTIONAL OBSERVATIONS?	HOW DO THESE BIASES SHOW UP DURING INSTRUCTIONAL OBSERVATIONS?	HOW DO THESE BIASES SHOW UP DURING FEEDBACK CYCLES AND SETTING GOALS WITH TEACHERS?
Affinity Bias			
Attribution Bias			
Confirmation Bias			
Cultural Bias			

3. **Calibrate Observations Frequently to Ensure Consistency:** With the presence of a systemwide framework describing teaching practice, an important step in your endeavors to support teachers is to ensure everyone utilizing the framework applies it consistently. This requires those observing instruction to periodically calibrate together by conducting observations of the same teacher(s) and determining performance levels together. Engaging in this practice often illuminates the presence of the unconscious bias, which allows observers to then recenter their work on the explicit language in the framework. Even more importantly, periodic calibration amongst evaluators ensures the validity of any data gathered from performance levels that may inform high-stakes decisions such as planning continuous improvement efforts. In all of these practices as the lead learner, you are modeling for teachers the willingness to engage in a cycle of personal inquiry in order to ensure you are utmost capable of serving them as a source of support in their own growth journey.

LEADING THE LEARNING THROUGH THE CONSCIOUS COMPETENCE MODEL

Understanding the science and impact of conscious competence as a lead learner is another extremely powerful move. According to early researcher Broadwell (1969), "In psychology, the four stages of competence, or the 'conscious competence' learning model, relates to the psychological states involved in the process of progressing from incompetence to competence in a skill. The four stages suggest that individuals are initially unaware of how little they know, or unconscious of their incompetence. As they recognize their incompetence, they consciously acquire a skill, then consciously use it. Eventually, the skill can be utilized without it being consciously thought through: the individual is said to have then acquired unconscious competence" (para. 6).

In addition, there is a myth in the field of education that all teachers need to be and should be good at everything they are asked to do. However, with the national shortage in teachers and teacher prep programs, we are seeing more and more teachers come into classrooms with little to no pedagogical or instructional experience to draw from. To complicate the educational landscape even more, we have an influx of new administrators that are being asked to coach up new and veteran teachers with instructional practices, methods, and pedagogy.

This is an incredibly challenging task for all administrators. Understanding the science of learning and how the four stages of learning, or Conscious Competence Matrix (see Figure 5.2), impacts adult learning is essential when trying to train and scale instructional best practices and methods within your school system.

Figure 5.2 shows the Conscious Competence Matrix, which can be used to more deeply understand the four stages of learning.

FIGURE 5.2 ● Conscious Competence Matrix

UNCONSCIOUS INCOMPETENCE	CONSCIOUS INCOMPETENCE
Mindset: We don't know what we don't know. **Culture:** Educators may deny using new resources or need for quality curriculum, methods, and instructional practices. They are very comfortable with the status quo.	**Mindset:** We know what we don't know. **Culture:** Educators may be very uncomfortable or feel vulnerable because they are aware that they are not competent in using new resources or instructional methods. This stage can be the most challenging because emotions can run high when people do not feel confident in what they are doing.
CONSCIOUS COMPETENCE	**UNCONSCIOUS COMPETENCE**
Mindset: We know what we are improving and working on. We use that as a personalized goal. **Culture:** The growth mindset is alive and well in this domain. Teachers feel supported in their learning and know they can be vulnerable, but they are starting to gain confidence and skills that they notice are working well for them.	**Mindset:** We know something so well that it is automatic, or we don't have to think about it. **Culture:** A growth mindset is key in this domain. Teachers are using new skills that are second nature to them, and they might be thinking about getting coaching to learn something new again based on their confidence and competence. Teachers are typically asking for feedback and wanting to set new goals because of the success they have had learning new skills or resources.

IF YOUR TEAM IS DEMONSTRATING . . .	FOCUS ON SUPPORTING THEM BY. . . .
Unconscious Incompetence	Building trusting relationships so that educators can remove any armor they may have; listen to feedback; and, with your support, set their own personalized learning goals.
Conscious Incompetence	This stage can be the most challenging for everyone involved. Teachers may feel insecure of their incompetence and need both pedagogical methods and instructional skills, but also emotional support as they are uncomfortable with their learning cycle. Be prepared to support them with professional learning experiences that meet their differentiated needs.

IF YOUR TEAM IS DEMONSTRATING ...	FOCUS ON SUPPORTING THEM BY....
Conscious Competence	Continue to support teachers with differentiated strategies and provide opportunities for them to reflect on what they are doing and why. This will help move them into Unconscious Competence quicker.
Unconscious Competence	Provide opportunities for educators to share their skills with others who are in the conscious competence stage. Creating an environment where everyone is in this conscious competence cycle while potentially working on different personalized learning goals will help develop a positive learning culture for adult learners.

As a lead learner, using the conscious competence matrix to model an area of growth you are working on will help reinforce that you are creating a safe learning environment for adult and student learners. Making sure you are sharing your growth and leveraging language around conscious competence will show that your actions match your high expectations for all adult learners. Using the Conscious Competence Matrix as a lead learner will provide a framework and mental model to reinforce the growth mindset that is crucial for adult learners to rumble with and embrace.

The Big Ideas

In this chapter, we identified that being a learner is a key tenant of leadership. Showing up in front of your staff as a learner and not just an evaluator supports a culture of vulnerability, a growth mindset, and conscious competence culture. You also explored how lead learners show up in Professional Learning Communities, instructional rounds, and planning for professional learning. Lead learners are vulnerable with their staff and are curious when reflecting about how affinity bias, attribution bias, confirmation bias, and cultural bias may impact them as a leader. Chapter 5 highlighted that great leaders are inherently life-long learners.

Let's Reflect

1. As a lead learner, what are your own professional goals for the next month, quarter, and year?

   _____

   _____

   _____

2. Who might you want to collaborate with as a thinking partner to help you identify your unconscious competence? When thinking about being vulnerable and not knowing everything as the leader of your team, what emotions does that bring up for you?

   _____

   _____

   _____

3. How will the vision of your district or school impact your own learning goals and professional learning? What support will you need and seek out?

   _____

   _____

   _____

4. How will you share and model for your staff your learning as a leader?

   _____

   _____

   _____

What's Next?

In Chapter 6, we will investigate the habit of having high expectations for all. Few leaders will assert that they start each school day with the intent to lower expectations for teachers and students. However, in a contemporary education environment with challenging staff retention concerns and unclear pathways toward addressing student learning interruptions, leaders may be at risk for inadvertently allowing a slow, gentle decline in expectations of their community that can have devastating cumulative effects. We frame this behavior as *loving the school into failure*. This chapter will provide strategies for building team maturity and understanding around the causes and effects of adult expectations, examine the effect of martyrdom in a school setting, and offer tools for learning to *give away the work* so others may become equal owners of the impact. While the habit of being a lead learner is very distinct and unique, you will see that there are places where the habit of high expectation intersects, especially when thinking through biases and mindsets.

CHAPTER 6

High Expectations for All

Samantha, a new high school principal, was observing a data driven PLC (professional learning community.) As Samantha observed, she noticed a few veteran teachers were presenting the data and making all of the instructional connections and decisions. Several of the teachers in the PLC appeared disengaged and were not participating in the dialogue. It was evident there was no shared ownership. Samantha noticed the teachers not participating were disengaged verbally and nonverbally. One teacher was on her phone texting throughout the entire meeting. Furthermore, during instructional rounds, Samantha had noticed teachers were not even working on common standards. It was evident based on her instructional rounds and observation of their data driven dialogue that the team was not working collectively and that some of the teachers were coasting off the coattails of their colleagues. Samantha recognized the demanding work a few of the teachers were putting into planning but wanted to ensure all teachers were contributing. Also, Samantha noticed that the teachers needed some support with team maturity when it came to collaboration and calibration. She grappled with the fact that the team did not have team norms, nor did they have clear roles and responsibilities or any verbal or nonverbal expectations for themselves or one another during the PLC. It was evident high expectations for all were needing to be clarified and that Samantha needed to coach the team with what she expected from each of them.

WHY PRACTICE THE HABIT
OF HIGH EXPECTATIONS FOR ALL

In the context of educational leadership, the term "high expectations" embodies the belief that all adult scholars are capable of learning at elevated levels. For those in leadership positions, particularly as transformational and instructional leaders, upholding high expectations requires ensuring that academic rigor and resources support the delivery of quality education. Ultimately, leaders carry the responsibility of establishing the standard of expectations for both their staff and students. To facilitate the cultivation of a high-expectations culture, leaders should offer professional development opportunities and guidance on content, pedagogy, and instructional methods tailored to specific subjects or grade levels.

It is crucial for leaders to identify and remove barriers that impede educator performance, such as lack of resources, insufficient professional learning opportunities, absence of support systems like instructional coaching, and unclear expectations regarding attendance for both staff and students. Establishing norms and procedures for effective collaboration and communication within professional learning communities is vital in fostering a conducive work culture and elevating performance levels.

It is crucial for leaders to identify and remove barriers that impede educator performance, such as lack of resources, insufficient professional learning opportunities, absence of support systems like instructional coaching, and unclear expectations regarding attendance for both staff and students.

Moreover, leaders must uphold high expectations for communication among students, families, and educators. Modeling and expecting excellence in verbal and nonverbal communication from all stakeholders can significantly influence the overall school culture in either a positive or negative manner. "The key to creating a high-expectations culture is to understand that 'high expectations' is both believing in the capabilities of the adult and students in your building—and engaging in the actions that turn those beliefs into truth" (New Leaders, n.d.).

By instilling a culture of excellence through high expectations, leaders set a standard for performance and behavior that communicates a message of rejecting mediocrity. Encouraging students and teachers to surpass their comfort zones and strive for excellence not only enhances individual achievements but also enhances the overall quality of education within the school. Holding high expectations for all educators and scholars is a

FIGURE 6.1 ● Characteristics of High Expectations for All Educators

WHAT HIGH EXPECTATION FOR ALL EDUCATORS IS	WHAT HIGH EXPECTATION FOR ALL EDUCATORS IS NOT
Believing all educators can learn and grow in pedagogy, instructional practices, and methods	Believing that some educators have difficulties and are not coachable
Embracing the mantra "I will use a different strategy with my adult learners"	Embracing the mantra, "I give up, these teachers are too difficult for me to reach"
Understanding instructional coaching is a pathway to growing mastery in all educators	Feeling that instructional coaching is fruitless and the educator is unmotivated and lacks experience, classroom management, and pedagogy
Providing rigorous and challenging tasks for all educators that push them to think critically and creatively	Using high expectations as a means to punish or shame educators for not meeting goals
Offering regular, constructive feedback to help educators improve and understand their progress	Expecting educators to meet high standards without providing the necessary resources, guidance, and encouragement
Believing all educators are capable of using verbal and nonverbal strategies to communicate professionally	Making excuses for educators when they do not use professional verbal and nonverbal skills with other staff, students, or families

critical habit for leaders to prioritize, as it plays a significant role in shaping the trajectory of success at various levels within an academic institution (see Figure 6.1).

HOW TEAM MATURITY AND COLLECTIVE TEACHER EFFICACY AFFECTS HIGH EXPECTATIONS

Countless books, blogs, and research have gone into developing effective and efficient teams. As educational leaders, we know within a few minutes of observing a team if they are highly effective and efficient or incompetent and oppositional. Often the biggest challenge transformation and instructional leaders have is identifying the phase of maturation of a team which will lead to collective teacher efficacy. John Hattie has written numerous books and research articles on the effect size that collective teacher efficacy has on student growth and achievement. Hattie's meta research has indicated that collective efficacy has a 1.34 effect size on student achievement (Hattie et al., 2024). Meaning, when John Hattie uses the term "effect size," he can measure how much an educational strategy or intervention influences student learning. Effect size is like a yardstick that helps educators understand the impact of different teaching methods. Hattie developed a way to compare and rank these influences based on their effect sizes, which are calculated using a standard metric called Cohen's d. By doing this, Hattie can highlight which strategies have the strongest positive impact on student learning and which ones may have a negative effect. This approach provides educators and policymakers with valuable information on what works best in improving educational outcomes for students (Hattie, 2015).

Therefore, because collective teacher efficacy has one of the highest effect sizes this warrants leaders spending time being curious and developing trust and team maturity within their grade level and content level teams. "There is a reciprocal relationship between individual and collective efficacy. As one gets stronger, so does the other. Stronger collective efficacy seems to encourage individual teachers to make more effective use of the skills they already have. And strong individual efficacy allows teams to function more productively" (Hoy et al., 2002, p. 14). Unfortunately, simply telling a team of educators to share knowledge and resources doesn't typically work well. Hattie's research also indicates that teacher trust plays into teacher influence and impact.

However, with the hustle and bustle of new school years, taking time to build trusting relationships within teams and with school leaders often gets overlooked. Using research-based resources and theories like Bruce Tuckman's Team Maturity Theory (Tuckman, 1965), leaders can more easily identify, support, and develop the stages or phases of team maturity, which leads to collective teacher efficacy. Tuckman's stages of group development include the following steps:

- forming
- storming
- norming
- performing
- adjourning

One thing to be aware of when using this maturity matrix is that it is more cyclical than linear. All of the team maturity phases are necessary and inevitable in order for a team to grow, accept challenges, rumble with problems, find solutions, collectively plan work, and deliver results for all learners. The end goal is collective teacher efficacy, but without support, this is very difficult to truly achieve.

The Team Maturity Matrix in Figure 6.2 can help you when observing team meetings or professional learning communities. Identify the specific phase a team may be emulating. Next, use evidence from the observation and Team Maturity Matrix to communicate the challenges and opportunities that come with team development and the support you plan to provide them as they move through the various stages.

FIGURE 6.2 ● Team Maturity Matrix

Phase 1	**Forming attributes:** This is the beginning stage where a team is initially coming together. Members are getting to know each other and understanding their roles and responsibilities. Norms and roles are determined by all stakeholders in this phase.	**Forming mindsets or cultures to notice:** Communication and expectations are set by those who have previously been on the team. Not all voices are seen, heard, and valued.
Phase 2	**Storming attributes:** The second phase, where conflicts and disagreements may arise as team members start to push against the boundaries established in the forming stage. This is a critical phase for growth as it helps to address and resolve differences.	**Storming mindsets or cultures to notice:** Participants do not communicate, they operate in silos, do not share, do not cooperate, and they are interested in their own outcome and needs. Emotionally you may notice unwelcoming culture and a focus on the individual not the collective group.
Phase 3	**Norming attributes:** The team begins to establish norms and standards for how they will work together. Roles become clearer, and the team starts to work more cohesively.	**Norming mindsets or cultures to notice:** Increased communication and high expectations are being established verbally and nonverbally within the team. Constructive debate and dialogue is starting to take place by all voices on the team.
Phase 4	**Performing attributes:** The team reaches a high level of performance, working efficiently toward their goals. Collaboration is strong, and the team can handle complex tasks and challenges effectively.	**Performing mindsets or cultures to notice:** Trust has been built, and there is collaboration, partnership, collective work, and support for one another. This is evident through both verbal and nonverbal communication. Empathy, acknowledgement of mistakes, and accepting others are evident.
Stage 5	**Adjourning attributes:** This final stage occurs when the team has completed its goals and may disband. It's a time for reflection and celebration of the team's achievements.	**Adjourning mindsets and cultures to notice:** Student focus, purposeful dialogue and practice, empowerment, and ownership by all team members exist. This is evident through both verbal and nonverbal communication. There is a determination to succeed together.

HOW VERBAL AND NONVERBAL COMMUNICATION AFFECTS HIGH EXPECTATIONS

Verbal and nonverbal communication skills are both crucial for positive school culture and effective leadership. Some key communication aspects that can impact effective communication are as follows:

- body language
- tone
- facial expressions
- clear and precise language (especially when providing direction, vision, feedback, and guidance)

However, it is important to remember that communication is a two-way experience. Good leaders are able to communicate their thoughts and vision but are also active listeners. "They don't just listen to the comments and feedback from their team; they process, retain, discuss, and, if possible, incorporate it into the decision-making process. When team members feel like they are heard, it builds morale" (Patel, 2024, p. 52). No doubt, communication is a very complex and challenging aspect of school and district leadership. Therefore, another area that leaders must observe and commit to addressing is how all stakeholders—students, staff, and families—communicate with one another. High expectations for one group and not another will quickly create an environment where not all voices feel seen, heard, and valued. For example, having high expectations for teachers to use effective verbal and nonverbal communication with all stakeholders and then letting an angry parent berate a teacher in front of you will send a message to your staff that you have high expectations for them but do not care about how they are treated by others. In addition, as a leader it is important to focus on how you communicate verbally and nonverbally, but you must be able to also observe verbal and nonverbal cues of your stakeholders. When observing professional learning communities or parent-teacher, student-teacher, teacher-teacher, or student-student interactions, leaders must be able to decipher the verbal and nonverbal cues of others. "This skill, often referred to as 'emotional intelligence,' enables a leader to gauge the mood, feelings, and sometimes even the unspoken concerns of their team members. By staying attuned to subtle shifts in body language, facial expressions, and even the dynamics of how space is used, a leader can address potential issues before they escalate and adapt their approach to meet the emotional and psychological needs of their team" (Thought Collective, 2023). It is of utmost importance that when you are focusing on communication, that you communicate and follow-up with high expectations for all stakeholders and not just one group of people. Use Figure 6.3 to determine your own strengths and areas that you might want to set as a focus goal. You can also use the chart to help staff determine their collective strengths and an area they want as a focus goal:

FIGURE 6.3 ● Effective Verbal and Nonverbal Communication Evaluation Tool

VERBAL COMMUNICATION	SCORE 1–5 (1 BEING THE LOWEST AND 5 THE HIGHEST)	NONVERBAL COMMUNICATION	SCORE 1–5 (1 BEING THE LOWEST AND 5 THE HIGHEST)
Information is conveyed concisely and clearly.		Awareness of body posture (Do you look tired, excited, bored, engaged?)	
Language is culturally responsive.		Awareness of paralinguistics or tone of voice (calm, angry, condescending, kind)	
Clear articulation and enunciation.		Awareness of facial expression (warm, cool, smiling)	
Listening skills, you are not just talking at someone, but respecting them and inviting them into the conversation.		Awareness of eye contact (Are you looking kindly into someone's eyes, squinting in frustration, or avoiding eye contact all together?)	
Repeat what you heard back for clarification. "I heard you say . . . is that correct?"		Awareness of proxemics or personal space (Sitting at a desk in the office while talking to stakeholders can send a message of dominance and power.)	
Determine whether you should use formal or informal language and vocabulary based on the audience you are speaking with.		Awareness of haptics or touch (Do others feel physically safe with a handshake or pat on the back?)	

Good leaders are able to communicate their thoughts and vision but are also active listeners.

In the realm of high expectations and leadership, the power of verbal and nonverbal communication cannot be overemphasized. As we have explored, the nuances of verbal and nonverbal communication skills play a pivotal role in reinforcing messages, building rapport, and ultimately, in shaping perceptions. However, "the effective use of nonverbal cues by leaders can bridge the gap between mere words and the conveyance of emotions and intentions, creating a more profound impact on their audience. As we move forward, let us hold on to the curiosity that drives us to delve deeper into the unspoken, recognizing its potential to transform the very essence of leadership" (Thought Collective, 2023, p. 26).

Pause and Reflect

Reflect using this graphic organizer to describe ways you have noticed nonverbal communication impacting high expectations.

Describe a time you observed nonverbal communication that either motivated or hindered the motivation of staff, students, and/or families.	
How did that nonverbal communication impact the culture of the environment?	
What area of nonverbal communication do you think is a strength of yours? What is an area of growth that you would like to focus on?	
How do you provide feedback that supports high expectations in nonverbal communication? What support do you need to ensure you are providing follow-up and feedback?	

HIGH EXPECTATIONS AND ATTENDANCE OF STAFF AND STUDENTS

Educators and scholars are experiencing high levels of stress. Compound these mental health challenges with increasing demands on teaching and learning, implementations of new curriculum, technology, and instructional practices and most educators and scholars are feeling overwhelmed and burnt out. All of these challenges are contributing to staff and student absenteeism. First, we must acknowledge the overwhelm but not fall victim to lowering our expectations when it comes to staff and student school attendance.

Therefore, we must not lose sight in today's rapidly evolving world that education has become the foundation for success and personal development. To ensure an optimal learning environment, it is crucial to establish high expectations concerning school attendance for both staff and students. By fostering a mindset that prioritizes attendance, we can cultivate a culture of commitment and achievement. High attendance expectations serve as a catalyst for academic excellence. Regular attendance allows students to benefit from consistent instruction, engage actively in classroom discussions, and maintain a coherent understanding of the curriculum. By attending school regularly, students can establish a regular study routine, thereby enhancing their chances of academic success. Additionally, high attendance expectations provide an opportunity for educators to provide targeted support and individualized instruction, leading to improved academic outcomes.

Having high expectations regarding school attendance for staff and students cultivates a strong work ethic. When students are expected to attend regularly, they develop a sense of dedication and self-motivation toward their studies. Similarly, educators who uphold high attendance expectations demonstrate their commitment to providing quality education and become role models for their students. This collective effort fosters a positive work ethic within the entire school community, inspiring everyone to strive for excellence.

Establishing high attendance expectations strengthens the sense of community within schools. When everyone in the school community is committed to attending regularly, a positive and supportive atmosphere is created. Regular attendance allows students to form meaningful connections with their peers, teachers, and staff. This sense of belonging creates a conducive environment for social-emotional growth, collaboration, and empathy. Ultimately, a strong school community drives student engagement, school pride, and a collectively shared responsibility for success.

Life is full of challenges and unpredictability. By prioritizing regular attendance, we equip staff and students with the resilience needed to face hardships that may arise. Consistently attending school exposes students to a diverse range of experiences, perspectives, and challenges. This dedication to showing up even during challenging times fosters adaptability, problem-solving skills, and the ability to overcome obstacles—traits that will prove invaluable as they navigate their future path(s).

Consistently attending school exposes students to a diverse range of experiences, perspectives, and challenges. This dedication to showing up even during challenging times fosters adaptability, problem-solving skills, and the ability to overcome obstacles—traits that will prove invaluable as they navigate their future path(s).

Pause and Reflect

Reflect on the following attendance action steps to determine which specific steps you need to take action on in order to ensure you are upholding high expectations for all stakeholders with attendance.

Attendance Action Steps Chart

Data Analysis and Monitoring

- Conduct a thorough analysis of attendance data to identify trends, patterns, and areas of concern.
- Utilize attendance tracking systems and tools to monitor and track student and staff attendance consistently.
- Set specific attendance goals and regularly review progress toward achieving those goals.

Our Current Reality:	Action Steps We Need to Take:

Establish Clear Attendance Policies

- Develop and communicate clear attendance policies for both students and staff, outlining expectations, consequences for non-attendance, and procedures for reporting absences.
- Ensure that attendance policies are consistent, easily accessible to all stakeholders, and aligned with district and state guidelines.

Our Current Reality:	Action Steps We Need to Take:

Collaborate With Families and Community Partners

- Engage with families to understand underlying reasons for absences and collaborate on solutions to improve attendance.
- Partner with community organizations, social services, and local agencies to provide support services and resources to address barriers to attendance, such as transportation issues or health-related concerns.

Our Current Reality:	Action Steps We Need to Take:

(Continued)

(Continued)

Implement Attendance Incentives and Recognition Programs

- Establish incentives and recognition programs to motivate students and staff to prioritize attendance.
- Recognize and celebrate individuals or classes with exceptional attendance records to reinforce the importance of regular attendance.

Our Current Reality:	Action Steps We Need to Take:

Provide Professional Development for Staff

- Offer professional development opportunities for educators on strategies to enhance student engagement, create a positive classroom environment, and address attendance issues effectively.
- Equip staff with tools and resources to support students who are facing attendance challenges and provide guidance on intervention strategies.

Our Current Reality:	Action Steps We Need to Take:

Conduct Attendance Awareness Campaigns

- Launch schoolwide attendance awareness campaigns to educate students, staff, and families about the significance of regular attendance.
- Use various communication channels, such as newsletters, announcements, and social media, to promote the importance of attendance and share tips on how to improve attendance habits.

Our Current Reality:	Action Steps We Need to Take:

Implement Early Intervention and Support Systems

- Develop early warning systems to identify students at risk of chronic absenteeism and provide targeted interventions to support their attendance.
- Establish a multitiered support system that includes counseling services, academic assistance, and mentorship programs to address the underlying causes of non-attendance.

Our Current Reality:	Action Steps We Need to Take:

Monitor and Evaluate Attendance Initiatives

- Regularly monitor the effectiveness of attendance initiatives, gather feedback from stakeholders, and make adjustments as needed.
- Utilize data analytics to track progress, measure the impact of interventions, and identify areas for improvement in addressing attendance issues.

Our Current Reality:	Action Steps We Need to Take:

SUPPORTING HIGH EXPECTATIONS THROUGH INSTRUCTIONAL COACHING SYSTEMS

Instructional coaching and leadership plays a crucial role in shaping the success and overall development of schools. One of the key elements of effective instructional coaching and leadership is setting high expectations for students, teachers, and the entire school community. High expectations foster a culture of excellence, motivate individuals to strive for greatness, and create an environment conducive to continuous improvement. When leaders set the bar high, they inspire students and teachers to believe in their abilities and work hard toward achieving their goals. In a study by Jussim and Harber (2005), the relationship between teacher expectations and student outcomes, including the impact on effort, engagement, and self-efficacy, was explored. The research indicated that high expectations consistently lead to increased effort, improved engagement, and a greater sense of self-efficacy. Educators who are challenged and believe in their ability to meet those challenges are more likely to persist in the face of obstacles and excel in the profession. As you endeavor to apply the habits of a lead learner that you explored in the previous chapter, consider the opportunity for enhancing the impact of PLCs, for example, when each participating educator feels both challenged and supported by your high expectations.

In schools, high expectations create an environment conducive to continuous improvement. When leaders set high standards, they encourage a mindset of constant growth and learning. Teachers are motivated to consistently evaluate their student's progress, identify areas for improvement, and seek opportunities for professional and personal development. In such an environment, failure is seen as a stepping stone to success rather than a roadblock. High expectations foster a commitment to ongoing improvement, allowing the school community to evolve and thrive.

When leaders set high standards for all educators, regardless of their teacher preparation training programs, or lack thereof, or personal circumstances, they send a powerful message that every educator is capable of success. By providing instructional coaching and support, leaders ensure that all educators have the opportunity to meet and exceed these expectations. Instructional coaching helps level the playing field, ensuring that every educator has access to a high-quality coach and professional learning, and provides educators with the necessary resources to succeed.

Figure 6.4 contains a framework for implementing and supporting instructional coaching. This tool can be used to help you and your team reflect and generate how you will support educators with professional learning and effective instructional coaching. By following the steps, a leader can successfully implement instructional coaching in a school setting, leading to improved teaching practices, increased student engagement and achievement, and a culture of continuous professional growth and learning.

FIGURE 6.4 ● A Framework for Implementing and Supporting Instructional Coaching

1. ASSESS THE NEEDS

The first step is to assess the needs of the teachers and the school as a whole. Identify areas where teachers may benefit from coaching support, such as implementing new instructional strategies, integrating technology into lessons, or differentiating instruction for diverse learners.

Things to Consider:

What tools are you using to assess the need (e.g., the Danielson Framework, which helps identify areas of strength and areas for support)?

2. DEVELOP A COACHING FRAMEWORK

Define a clear coaching framework that outlines the goals, expectations, and processes of instructional coaching. This framework should include the role of the coach, the frequency and duration of coaching sessions, and the methods for measuring progress and success.

Things to Consider:

What support is needed to help develop a coaching framework? Does the district have resources or do you need support (e.g., Visible Learning or Jim Knight's Coaching)?

3. RECRUIT AND TRAIN COACHES

Identify and train qualified educators to serve as instructional coaches. Coaches should have strong instructional skills, good communication abilities, and a supportive and nonjudgmental approach. Provide training on effective coaching strategies, communication techniques, and data analysis.

Things to Consider:

Who will train your instructional coaches? Where can you find support? There are many companies and independent consultants who offer instructional coaching. Make sure they have research-based experience before bringing them into your environment.

4. MATCH COACHES WITH TEACHERS

Match coaches with teachers based on their needs, goals, and personalities. It is important to establish a positive and trusting relationship between the coach and the teacher to ensure the success of the coaching process.

Things to Consider:

It is important to ensure that educators feel seen, valued, and heard by their coach. When possible, make sure the educators are involved in selecting their coaches.

(Continued)

(Continued)

5. SET GOALS AND ACTION PLANS

Collaborate with teachers and coaches to set clear, specific, and achievable goals for the coaching process. Develop action plans that outline the steps needed to achieve these goals, including timelines, resources, and strategies for monitoring progress.

Things to Consider:

As the school leader, you can guide the goals to align with the overall school vision or goals for the year. However, it is essential to let the educator and coach determine what and how these goals will be met and measured.

6. PROVIDE ONGOING SUPPORT

Offer ongoing support and resources to both coaches and teachers throughout the coaching process. Encourage open communication, provide feedback, and address any challenges or concerns that may arise.

Things to Consider:

School leaders should be updated about needs throughout the coaching process; however, they also need to honor the trusting relationship the two have built.

7. MONITOR AND EVALUATE PROGRESS

Regularly monitor and evaluate the progress of the coaching program. Collect data on teacher growth, student outcomes, and the overall impact of coaching on instruction. Use this data to make adjustments and improvements to the coaching process as needed.

Things to Consider:

What rubrics or resources will you use to evaluate the effectiveness of the instructional coaching in your building? How will you advocate for resources and support? Where and how will you share progress?

8. CELEBRATE SMALL MILESTONES

Celebrate and recognize the success and achievements of teachers who have participated in instructional coaching. Showcase examples of effective coaching outcomes and share success stories with the school community to inspire and motivate others.

Things to Consider:

Professional learning and growth can be very challenging work. It is essential that as the instructional leader you are part of celebrating the small milestones that your educators are accomplishing.

High expectations are crucial for effective instructional coaching in schools. They create a culture of excellence, motivate individuals to strive for greatness, and foster an environment of continuous improvement. Through setting high standards, instructional leaders instill a belief in teachers and students that they can achieve great things. By challenging individuals to exceed their perceived limitations, leaders pave the way for success and ensure that every student has the opportunity to reach their full potential.

The Big Ideas

In this chapter, we explored the significance of establishing high expectations as a foundational element in education, endorsing a belief in the inherent capabilities of all scholars to achieve at elevated levels and serving as a catalyst for creating a culture of excellence among staff and students. Our exploration included strategies aimed at cultivating team maturity and fostering a deep comprehension of the interconnected dynamics influencing adult expectations, emphasizing the profound impact that both verbal and nonverbal communication can have on shaping the culture and community within teams, classrooms, and the broader school environment. We highlighted the pivotal role of growth mindset, collective efficacy, and instructional coaching in enhancing the outcomes from upholding high expectations for all learners. Throughout the chapter, we underscored that the development of high expectations for educators is a nuanced and complex endeavor, requiring a mindful approach with an awareness of the multifaceted factors at play.

Let's Reflect

1. How do you model high expectations as an instructional leader in your building?

   _____

   _____

   _____

2. In what ways can schools and educational institutions enhance team maturity and promote a deep understanding of the interconnected dynamics influencing adult expectations to foster a culture of excellence?

   _____

   _____

   _____

   (Continued)

(Continued)

3. How do growth mindset, collective efficacy, and instructional coaching contribute to the outcomes derived from upholding high expectations for all learners, and what strategies can be implemented to leverage these factors effectively?

_____

_____

_____

4. What would you like to change?

_____

_____

_____

What's Next?

In Chapter 7, we will think about how data is crucial to the school or district leaders' ability to project needed efforts, measure impact of the work, and understand the myriad features of the school community. In addition, we will reflect on and define why an equitable approach for using data is important, as well as dig deeper into the relationship data has to the habit of high expectations for staff and students.

CHAPTER 7

Data Habits of an Evaluative Thinker

Juana was finishing her second year as a high school principal and counted the days remaining until she was able to take two weeks to go on a much-needed vacation. She was proud of all that had been accomplished in the prior year: implementing a new Career and Tech Education program in the school, hiring additional staff, and launching a new schoolwide social-emotional curriculum. Her district appeared to support her, and she had found some intriguing ideas through Internet searches and a recent leadership conference. Today, she opened the School Improvement Plan and began the tedious process of inputting data from dozens of sources. The platform required attendance data, student survey results, academic achievement and growth reports, total students qualifying for subsidized meals, teacher retention, and a host of other numbers, most of which she had never taken time to study. As the system regurgitated a form of an overall "score" according to state criteria, Juana was dismayed to see her school had declined in the two years of her leadership. She revisited her data points one at a time, culling information for hours to determine the source of this dropping score. While the school's attendance seemed to be improving, the emergent bilingual population of students' growth had fallen at an alarming rate. Then, she noticed her student survey results showed an exciting increase in the percentage of students who felt as though the adults at the school cared for and valued them. Now lost in a confusing maze of information, Juana was unsure where to focus her leadership for the coming year. What exactly was working well at the school, and what might be having a negative influence? She could rest confidently it was not for a lack of effort on the part of herself or her team, but she grappled with the realization that she had no clear understanding of whether, or why, any of their efforts were having any effect?

WHY MAKE A HABIT OF DATA USE

Data is all around you. As an education leader, you have likely been engaging with forms of data around the outcomes your school is achieving or areas where challenges are posed since the moment you began your role. Thinking about the development of your habits around data use in this chapter, however, is best understood in the context of your mindset and routines for becoming a skilled data-oriented practitioner. The more confident and comfortable you are in navigating the complex and diverse types of data available to you, the more likely you are to embrace its use as a routine form of practice to inform your leadership decisions.

The more confident and comfortable you are in navigating the complex and diverse types of data available to you, the more likely you are to embrace its use as a routine form of practice to inform your leadership decisions.

Researcher and professor John Hattie describes the concept of "evaluative thinking" as a mindset employed by high-impact instructional leaders who "believe their fundamental task is to evaluate the effect of everyone in their school on student learning" (Hattie, 2015). Evaluative thinking is described as "motivated by an attitude of inquisitiveness and a belief in the value of evidence" (Rickards et al., 2020, p. 89) and approached by "identifying assumptions, posing thoughtful questions, pursuing deeper understanding through reflection and perspective taking, and informing decisions in preparation for action" (Lu et al., 2019, p. 69). As leaders internalize the behaviors characterized by evaluative thinking, the habit of using data becomes as essential as the air you breathe. Evaluative thinking helps leaders move beyond surface-level conclusions toward using data, or evidence, to gain deeper insights about instructional practices, student learning, and organizational improvement. This type of thinking is fundamental to the approaches you learned in Chapter 4, "Check Your Blind Spots," for example. Hattie (2015) zeroes in on several specific mind frames of a leader who intentionally cultivates the habit of using data as an evaluative thinker, and the evidence strongly supports their effect on student learning outcomes. Two of the mind frames proven to have above-average effect sizes (ES) include the following:

- Leaders who believe their major role is to evaluate their impact (ES = .91)

- Leaders who get everyone in the school working together to know and evaluate their impact (ES = .91)

As you embark on the learning journey within this chapter, you'll explore the practices that hone your habits as a user of data who views their leadership through an evaluative thinkers' lens, perpetually curious and relentlessly in pursuit of evidence to understand the impact of your work. Consider the parallels and differences with your existing understanding as you examine Figure 7.1, describing effective data use in this context.

FIGURE 7.1 • Characteristics of Effective Data

EFFECTIVE DATA USE IS...	EFFECTIVE DATA USE IS NOT...
A fundamental component of a mindset of evaluative thinking wherein all stakeholders are constantly seeking to understand the impact of their work	Continuously gathering data from various sources without examining and analyzing it with purpose
Grounded in a mindset of inquiry, curiosity, and psychological safety	Regarded as an occasional *autopsy* approach to reflect backward on results from a narrow range of sources
Conducted across all areas of the system as viewed as a part of how all stakeholders routinely operate	Only conducted by leaders in isolated experiences Viewed by other stakeholders as something done *to* them instead of done *with* them
Routinely shared in various forms of communication with all stakeholders	Discoveries and findings never shared with the greater community

DATA HABITS THAT BUILD YOUR EVALUATIVE THINKING MUSCLE

Exploring specific mindsets and practices around using data is an important step toward becoming a skilled evaluative thinker who fosters a culture of inquiry for the entire community. Data will inform your efforts around the habit of upholding high expectations for all (Chapter 6), for example, as you gather measures of student learning. Where data may reveal some student subgroups are exceeding typical growth, for example, and others are falling far short of comparative norms can invite an important exploration of what impact various instructional practices and resources are having. Without a deep understanding of the mindsets that enable a community to approach data with curiosity and objectivity as opposed to fear and anxiety, meaningful and impactful changes in practice that influence the differences in student growth are unlikely to occur. Throughout the chapter, you'll examine strategies for building the habits of recognizing data sources and developing a community of thriving, growth-focused evaluative thinkers.

UNDERSTAND YOUR DATA MINES

As you learned in Chapter 4, data can offer an important opportunity to dispel myths, mitigate the effect of bias (serving as a "bias buster"), disrupt patterns of negative behavior, inform critical leadership decisions, and much more. Without data, you will always be at risk for subjecting your community to time loss, skewed or inaccurate opinions, and vague or unclear understanding of the system's meaningful growth toward achieving the purpose you examined in Chapter 3. Experts Wellman and Lipton (2017), authors of *Data Driven Dialogue, 2nd ed.*, assert "data are necessary to calibrate perception" (p. 67). Thus, an important beginning stage of your data journey must begin with addressing the question, "what data?" Figure 7.2 describes various sources of data available to education leaders that pertain to evaluating the impact of a diverse range of leadership practices. Compare them against data you are familiar with having previously gathered in any capacity, and use the empty spaces to document new ideas you may have for data sources specific to your setting.

FIGURE 7.2 ● Common Data Sources for Leaders

DATA TYPE	EXAMPLE(S)	THIS DATA MAY ASSIST ME TO . . .	DATA OF THIS TYPE I MIGHT GATHER . . .
Student learning data	**Quantitative sources:** assessment results of any kind (formative, summative, state assessments, benchmark assessments, etc.) **Qualitative sources:** portfolios of student work, presentations, teacher observational records, writing samples, etc.	Measure and observe student acquisition of knowledge and conceptual understandings against established criteria. Identify teachers with strong instructional practices or in need of targeted support.	
School culture data	Staff and student attendance records Student experience surveys (e.g., reporting on safety)	Triangulate student learning data for increased understanding of different areas influencing outcomes.	

DATA TYPE	EXAMPLE(S)	THIS DATA MAY ASSIST ME TO ...	DATA OF THIS TYPE I MIGHT GATHER ...
	Behavior records (e.g., suspensions) Family engagement data	Mitigate unconscious bias about specific populations of students or families (an application of the skills described in Chapter 4, "Check Your Blind Spots").	
Perception data	Surveys administered to stakeholder groups School score cards developed from community ratings Interviews with stakeholders or community members	Enhance understanding of the impact leadership efforts have on community engagement with the school (enabling you to more effectively cast your vision as described in Chapter 3). Determine new opportunities to meet unique needs of different stakeholders.	
Program data	Acceptance rates into next levels or post-secondary programs Participation in specific courses or programs Family attendance at community outreach events	Identify the merit of continuing or changing program implementation based on outcomes. Promoting specific programs to new audiences with data to substantiate their value.	
Community data	Demographic information on community members (family income, home language, etc.) Types of external support provided by community groups Media coverage	Identifying new avenues for funding or collaboration with external organizations to more fully meet student needs. More effectively incorporating all stakeholders into the school's journey toward the vision.	

With a broader perspective on the types and sources of data you may gather to evaluate your impact across a variety of areas of your work, you are equipped to begin the process of interpretation. Remembering that "evaluative thinking involves invoking reasoning and critical thinking in valuing evidence, leading to where-to-next recommendations" (Hattie, 2023, para. 2), the experience of analyzing and determining the nuanced messages gleaned from within the data will guide subsequent decisions and actions. To do so requires developing meaningful questions that promote responding, not reacting, to the data.

ASK QUESTIONS THAT PROMOTE EVALUATIVE THINKING

For education leaders, becoming an evaluative thinker means asking questions that don't simply seek answers but invite deeper exploration, encourage reflection on practice, and challenge assumptions. To develop this habit, leaders must become more intentional about their questions, ensuring they are rooted in evidence and aimed at enhancing understanding rather than confirming biases or seeking quick solutions. Hattie describes this approach as one of the critical mind frames of a leader who has a high impact on student learning outcomes, emphasizing the importance of routinely "addressing the fidelity of implementation, continually checking for unintended consequences, and allowing for adaptations to maximize the value of the outcomes" (Hattie, 2023, para. 3). Asking questions that require data to answer and are framed in terms of impact helps a team of educators to develop a habit of evaluative thinking. Questions can be designed to require evidence to guide improvements rather than gut feelings, assumptions, or anecdotal experiences. For example, questions that promote evaluative thinking focus not just on what strategies or methods are being used but on their impact on student learning. Notice the opportunity to deepen your impact as a lead learner using such questions with the practices described in Chapter 5!

As you are designing questions to apply in data conversations with your stakeholders—staff, students, families, etc.—be aware of the inclination to infuse your question with the preexisting belief or idea you already hold. Consider the question, "What could the Grade 7 teachers have done differently this year to see more significant growth on the end of year assessment?" The incorporation of the idea that something *could* be done differently implies that something *should* have been done differently. And perhaps that may be true! However, the listener will likely develop their response now in a manner that either complies with the implication to appease you or defies the implication and then rests in a defensive mindset for the remainder of the conversation. Instead, the question could be formulated like this, "What new ideas have you gleaned from the grade-level growth data about what strategies worked well this year, and what might be areas you'll reconsider in the future?" Using language that promotes widely diverse responses derived fully from the responder's personal reflections and ideas is described as inquiry-based questioning—questions that may promote more questions, for example, where no single individual is presumed to hold all the answers. Consider these examples and the way of thinking they invite from the responder:

- What patterns are we seeing in our student achievement data, and what questions does this raise about our current teaching practices?

- What evidence do we have that this teaching strategy is making a difference in student outcomes?

- What assumptions are we making about how students learn, and how might those assumptions be affecting our teaching practices?

- How can we work together to address the specific challenges we're seeing with student engagement?

- What challenges could arise if we shift to this new grading system? or What are some questions we haven't yet considered about this policy?

Another specific strategy can be to start with an undisputable fact (nonjudgemental and objective information), such as "our attendance has dipped in the 10th grade," followed by an invitation to collaboratively explore, notice, and wonder: "Let's dig into why that might be happening. What patterns are we noticing?" To further the curiosity-driven approach, follow-up with, "What questions does this bring up for us? How can we explore this further?" which promote a team approach to solving problems and encourage the sharing of ideas and strategies.

> *Using language that promotes widely diverse responses derived fully from the responder's personal reflections and ideas is described as inquiry-based questioning—questions that may promote more questions, for example, where no single individual is presumed to hold all the answers.*

No matter the data of focus, if your intent is to cultivate curiosity in others as a leader, modeling this behavior and approach to questioning is essential. Framing your questions about the data at hand in this way offers a powerful opportunity to shape the experiences of any stakeholder with whom you are engaging to experience trust, psychological safety, and the courage to boldly share new ideas.

Pause and Reflect

How might you apply the question-design strategies described here in a future experience with stakeholders where data is being examined and explored?

_____

_____

_____

_____

_____

LEADING A COMMUNITY OF DATA HUNTERS

As a leader, you may often feel the pressure to have all the answers or to always be responsible for solving problems. Simultaneously, you may strive to instill in others a mindset oriented toward growth and curiosity that rests on dispelling assumptions and mitigating the effect of unconscious bias. For example, while you endeavor to drive the focus of your leadership team's decision around selecting a new benchmark assessment tool, you experience the need to assert the exact merits and limits of the various options from your own knowledge base. However, to do so is likely to significantly influence the opinions of your team as they navigate their own need to align with your decisions, avoid friction by rejecting your opinions, or demonstrate their own competence by agreeing with you despite not having all the needed information. For a healthy culture of evaluative thinking to become embedded throughout your stakeholder community and to create a true culture of inquiry, it's incumbent on you to intentionally make space for uncertainty. And for data use to feel as though it's a normal part of such a culture, words and actions are an important component of how you convey the merit of curiosity and the pursuit of continuous improvement. Too often, educator communities are at risk for experiencing the weaponization of data, or the attribution of fixed and permanent characteristics to individuals and groups described by the data in a deficit-oriented manner. Here are some practices that a leader of a community of evaluative thinkers who experience confidence, psychological safety, and efficacy can use as they explore and utilize data:

For a healthy culture of evaluative thinking to become embedded throughout your stakeholder community and to create a true culture of inquiry, it's incumbent on you to intentionally make space for uncertainty.

Go on a Treasure Hunt, not a Witch Hunt: So often when educators at any level examine data, the inclination is to zero in on the lowest numbers, the declines over time, or the specific groups that fall below the norm. It's easy to lose sight of the data that reveal where there were positive trends, or to rest on the assumption that those data sets exist because of preexisting factors that enable certain groups to succeed no matter the conditions or influential factors. This is a missed opportunity! As you lead your community toward embracing all forms of data and the interpretations they necessitate, begin these experiences with fidelity to seek out strengths, positive changes, or positive outliers as a way of finding *treasure* amidst the entire collection of evidence. Remember that data from different sources may also merit unpacking further to discern these highlights. For example, benchmark assessment results in grade-level math may lead teachers to describe an entire group of students with relatively lower scores as their "low kiddos" or "low babies," a vast generalization for an enormously complex subject. Shift the conversation to focus on individuals or small groups within the results who demonstrate higher relative proficiency in a specific standard or instructional area.

Focus on Positive Outliers, and Replicate Powerful Practices: With a focus on finding strengths within a pool of data, you're on your way to specifically noticing the presence of positive outliers. Don't stop there! Just as you would analyze the lowest data set to determine how to respond with interventions, notice that the positive outliers may be the result of previously applied interventions or other powerful practices. To dismiss these outliers as the result of luck, demographics, personal traits, or other areas out of a teacher's control is to support the myth that the classroom teacher does not influence the data whether it's positive or negative. Rather, attend equally as much effort and thought to identifying the potential root causes for why the positive outlier data sets exist. When analyzing data as a group, for example, take the conversation to the classroom! Observe instruction in the settings where the positive outlier data sets exist. Generate collective understandings about what may have caused the success: instructional strategies? resources? schedule? As you refine understanding about likely influences, amplify the likelihood of others benefitting from them and seek to replicate these powerful practices in other settings across the school.

Face Data Fears: For any educator in any role, data may feel at times as though it is an indictment of proof that confirms negative beliefs, theories, or perceptions. The education profession, like many others, may also involve deeply personal and emotional connections to the work that put you at risk for significant disappointment or stress in the face of data that highlights subpar outcomes or failure to meet an established expectation. Like a grief cycle, you may experience a range of emotions in reaction to data from denial to anger or even bargaining. Further, you may develop unconscious fear of data that affirms something unpleasant or challenging. As the leader of a community of evaluative thinkers, however, it's incumbent on you to face your data fears and model for others that all data is simply information that serves to inform how we respond and move forward. As a first step, consider the learning experiences in Chapter 4 on checking your blind spots and take time to determine what data fears—a type of blind spot—you may have. Notice that "evaluative thinking involves investigating potential biases and confounding factors that may lead to false conclusions" (Hattie, 2023, para. 2). By modeling for your community a process for unpacking hidden emotions you may possess related to some forms of data, or unconscious biases you experience that lead you to only investigate data that affirms your preexisting beliefs, for example, you create an environment that is safe for others to do the same.

Give Away Your Power: Earlier you considered the notion that leaders are often expected—whether overtly or subconsciously—to have all the answers to challenges and problems. This is simply impossible. Another approach to modeling vulnerability and the mindset of curiosity, rather, is to give away your perceived problem-solving superpowers. For example, instead of moving to address the new mistake in the building's master schedule yourself, encourage others to ask questions and seek their own answers first. In experiences where you are positioned to be the group leader, such as team meetings, place your power in the hands of the group and seek and encourage input from all members. In a PLC, for example, you might ask, "What do we think is behind the drop in student engagement this month?" or "How might we better support our teachers who are feeling overwhelmed?" Not only will you be modeling the mindset you hope to develop in your team members, but you will glean valuable insight into the perspectives and opinions of the group that can maximize your ability to avoid unforeseen blind spots, too.

Another approach to modeling vulnerability and the mindset of curiosity, rather, is to give away your perceived problem-solving superpowers.

Conduct a Data Inventory: Schools are awash in immense amounts of data nearly all the time. You investigated strategies and mindsets for developing more effective questions earlier in the chapter, and a subsequent opportunity to even further deepen the value of those questions lies in examining and organizing the data types already available to you. Ultimately, you may then draw connections between the data sources in existence and the questions you aspire to address, but it's important to begin first with a data inventory. Documenting the myriad forms of data available can be guided with several parameters:

- Who is represented amongst the data sources (e.g., teachers, students, families, etc.)?
- Why has the data been collected?
- How often is the data collected?
- Who has access to the data?
- How can the data be categorized (e.g., qualitative vs. quantitative, or program vs. process vs. perception data)?

Following the initial organization of these responses, use this subset of questions to conduct an analysis:

- What data types do you most commonly focus on? Why might that be the case?
- Where are there "data deserts," or missing sources of data that may answer some of your key questions?
- Who is not represented in the data?
- Where might you connect the absence of some data types to the presence of blind spots?

As you apply any of these strategies in your context, recall the intent to cultivate your own mindset as well as that of your stakeholders around a collective pursuit of continuous improvement. Further, remember that a culture of evaluative thinking is not a program you implement—it's a way of thinking and being that should infuse everything your school does. From teacher evaluations to student projects, from administrative decisions to how you interact with families, the mindset of inquiry should be everywhere. How you incorporate data into this inquiry-driven approach will play a tremendous role in your success. When you consistently tie data use back to the greater purpose of enhancing outcomes for students, it becomes not just a requirement, but a shared responsibility and a source of pride. By laying a foundation of trust, curiosity, and shared purpose, you can lead your team to a place where data becomes an invaluable asset in driving meaningful, lasting change. Together, you and your community can develop a mindset that sees data not as a destination, but as a guide toward continuous improvement and collective success.

The Big Ideas

As an education leader, you have likely had immense experience with data in various ways throughout your career. Schools are systems that commonly implement intricate and complex processes for measuring all sorts of different things, yet data in and of itself is of little value without an effective mechanism and an informed mindset for utilizing it for a meaningful purpose. The power of data lies in what we do with it, or how we respond to it, rather than in the data itself. Expanding your perspective to also recognize that the value of data for leaders rests not only in your hands but in how you guide others to leverage the power of data to more accurately inform decisions at every level of the system. Nurturing and growing the data *health* of your stakeholders is a responsibility of education leaders to ensure that the community not only understands the story told by the data but that it embraces a culture of inquiry and curiosity.

As the habit of using data through the lenses described in this chapter becomes internalized for you, revisit earlier chapters such as "Leading the Learning" (Chapter 5) for an opportunity to apply new approaches to skills and practices that drive growth for every community member. Consider how data informs your responses and reactions to external influences that either cause you stress or promote your resilience and seek to replicate those sources that improve your well-being. Then, prepare to amplify your data-use habit even further in forthcoming chapters as you learn to pursue yet another form of data—feedback—to refine and enhance your efforts toward personal and professional growth.

Let's Reflect

1. What is your biggest challenge when it comes to using data effectively as a leader? How will you apply your learning to become more skilled in this habit?

   _____

   _____

   _____

2. Prior to reading this chapter, how would you characterize your typical mindset when approaching data use as a leader? What shifts have you noticed in this mindset as you examined the specific strategies and ideas around this habit?

   _____

   _____

   _____

3. What new ideas have you developed around the habit of using data to enhance your practice applying any of the prior chapter's habits (casting a vision, leading the learning, checking your blind spots, etc.)?

   _____

   _____

   _____

What's Next?

The skill of effectively using data as a leader extends well beyond solely examining the outcomes of student learning as the school year concludes. With your new mindset and practices around the habit of using data to more completely understand the ongoing journey of your school toward its vision, you will now shift to incorporating yet another form of data into your work: feedback. While feedback is commonly described as a form of information sharing between two entities (teacher to student, parent to school, supervisor to employee, etc.), the next habit zeroes in on the habit of leveraging feedback in a more personalized manner. As a leader, you are in a state of constantly receiving feedback, whether consciously or unaware. To grow and improve, understanding the input you gather all around you may have the effect of *tuning in* to the myriad opportunities for growth as you learn how others react to your decisions, ideas, and leadership style. Prepare to accelerate your growth and impact exponentially as you recognize the value of feedback of all types and forms and learn to intentionally seek and discover feedback along your leadership journey!

CHAPTER 8

Feedback Habits to Fuel Your Impact

Adam started his tenth year as a head of school with a feeling of mild skep-ticism that it would be a year any different than the past five, during which he had begun feeling as though he were "coasting" along in his career with ample success but little to inspire him for the future. There had been a time when his work felt fresh and new, and he was constantly pursuing new proj-ects and trying different ways of approaching the job. He had been proud of his reputation for being an innovator not only in his school but amongst several professional organizations as well. Now, as he settled into the rou-tines of starting the school year with his staff and visiting area schools to motivate the principals he supervised, he was annoyed with himself for feel-ing distracted and even bored. A colleague shared with him after a meeting one afternoon that he had just spent the most invigorating morning in a long session with his coach, and Adam was surprised—why would his friend, a veteran leader with even more experience than him in several well-respected districts, need a coach? He couldn't help but feel curious, and even a little jealous, at his friend's visible enthusiasm. Adam had never had a coach, nor could he even recall a time when he had someone give him meaningful feed-back or input about his own professional growth since he was a first-year teacher. Admittedly, he never saw much value in getting feedback, as he was wholly confident that he would not have risen to the role he held and achieved so many successes if he wasn't really good at his job. So what then, he wondered, was the big deal his colleague was so enthusiastic about after meeting with a coach, and what could he possibly need feedback on at this point in his career?

WHY FOCUS ON THE HABIT OF SEEKING FEEDBACK

Perhaps you are familiar with the immense amounts of attention paid in the education field to the skills and practices around giving effective feedback to others. Professional learning time is well spent when oriented toward leaders developing their ability to provide growth-focused feedback to teachers that enables them to enhance their impact in the classroom. And guiding teachers to learn the art of giving specific and actionable feedback to learners in the classroom is undoubtedly a valuable area of focus. Yet amidst the range of efforts focused on leaders providing feedback to others, rarely is there a shift of focus to recognize the value of seeking and applying feedback for yourself to continue to grow and thrive throughout your career. Without feedback, however, your learning and development is limited to narrow, siloed evidence of impact from only the sources near at hand or those you are accustomed to. By not actively seeking feedback, in fact, you are actively creating a sizeable blind spot with tremendous implications for limiting the trajectory of your career.

In her book *Impact Players*, Wiseman (2021) emphasizes the importance of actively seeking feedback as a key habit for personal and professional growth. Impact players—high-performing individuals—don't just passively wait for feedback; they actively seek it to improve their performance and ensure they're aligned with the organization's goals. This habit helps them recalibrate their efforts and stay focused on the most impactful tasks. Wiseman also highlights that feedback allows these individuals to adjust quickly to changing environments and challenges, rather than sticking to outdated methods. They approach feedback with a learner's mindset, seeking to correct mistakes and improve their contributions. This approach not only benefits their personal growth but also fosters innovation and agility within the organization, enabling them to stay ahead of the curve in dynamic workplaces.

By developing your own habit of seeking and utilizing feedback as a leader, you will become adept at identifying areas for improvement and innovation in response to changes, turning potential threats into opportunities. Embracing such a growth-oriented approach will allow you to make meaningful, sustained contributions, and you will serve as a model for the stakeholders in your community (those asked to both accept and provide feedback on a routine basis). You'll create an atmosphere where feedback is not feared but sought to enhance clarity, boost productivity, and foster collaboration. Leaders who engage in the routine practice of seeking feedback are not only going to experience personal growth but will support the growth of others by creating an environment where others feel seen, heard, and respected by their leader(s). Overall, your embodiment of evaluative thinking as it pertains to your impact as a leader will enable all stakeholders to recognize the vision that everyone in the community is responsible for driving student learning outcomes based on mutual input. Becoming comfortable and confident with the habit of seeking and using feedback as a leader, however, may not be as easy as it sounds thus far. Throughout this chapter, take careful note of your emotional reactions to the concepts and strategies. Consider where you may hold preexisting blind spots as discovered in Chapter 4 and recognize that the application of this habit is best viewed as a journey that may take time. Let's begin with an overview of what it means to employ effective feedback habits and dispel any myths you may hold around this habit (see Figure 8.1).

FIGURE 8.1 ● Characteristics of Effective Feedback Habits

EFFECTIVE FEEDBACK HABITS ARE . . .	EFFECTIVE FEEDBACK HABITS ARE NOT . . .
Proactive and growth-oriented, viewing feedback as input into a personal learning journey	Only applied in isolated settings when the feedback is likely to affirm existing beliefs or goals
A contributor to the overall community culture of psychological safety and collective focus on improvement	Experiences that put a leader at risk for seeming incapable or unprepared for the job
Explicitly aligned to areas in which you aspire to grow and improve, and clearly articulated as such to those providing feedback	Random or inconsistent, only sought following experiences of failure, tied only to external accountability measures such as district mandates
Iterative and ongoing for utmost impact, occurring in short-cycles while tied to either short- or long-term goals	Experienced in finite periods of time then abandoned and disconnected from current goals while continuing to "do what has always been done"

By developing your own habit of seeking and utilizing feedback as a leader, you will become adept at identifying areas for improvement and innovation in response to changes, turning potential threats into opportunities.

EXAMINING YOUR FEEDBACK MINDSETS

Developing a healthy mindset around seeking feedback is essential for your leadership work where growth, adaptability, and reflection are key. You may currently hold beliefs that feedback will undermine your authority or expose weaknesses. Or perhaps you consider yourself open to feedback, but your behavior does not demonstrate your beliefs, and you may have some blind spots about what it means to proactively seek feedback effectively. However, creating a culture where feedback is embraced rather than feared requires intentionality. It begins with viewing feedback not as a threat to our competence but as a valuable tool for growth. Before examining a range of distinct approaches, beliefs, and mindsets about feedback, complete the following reflection guide.

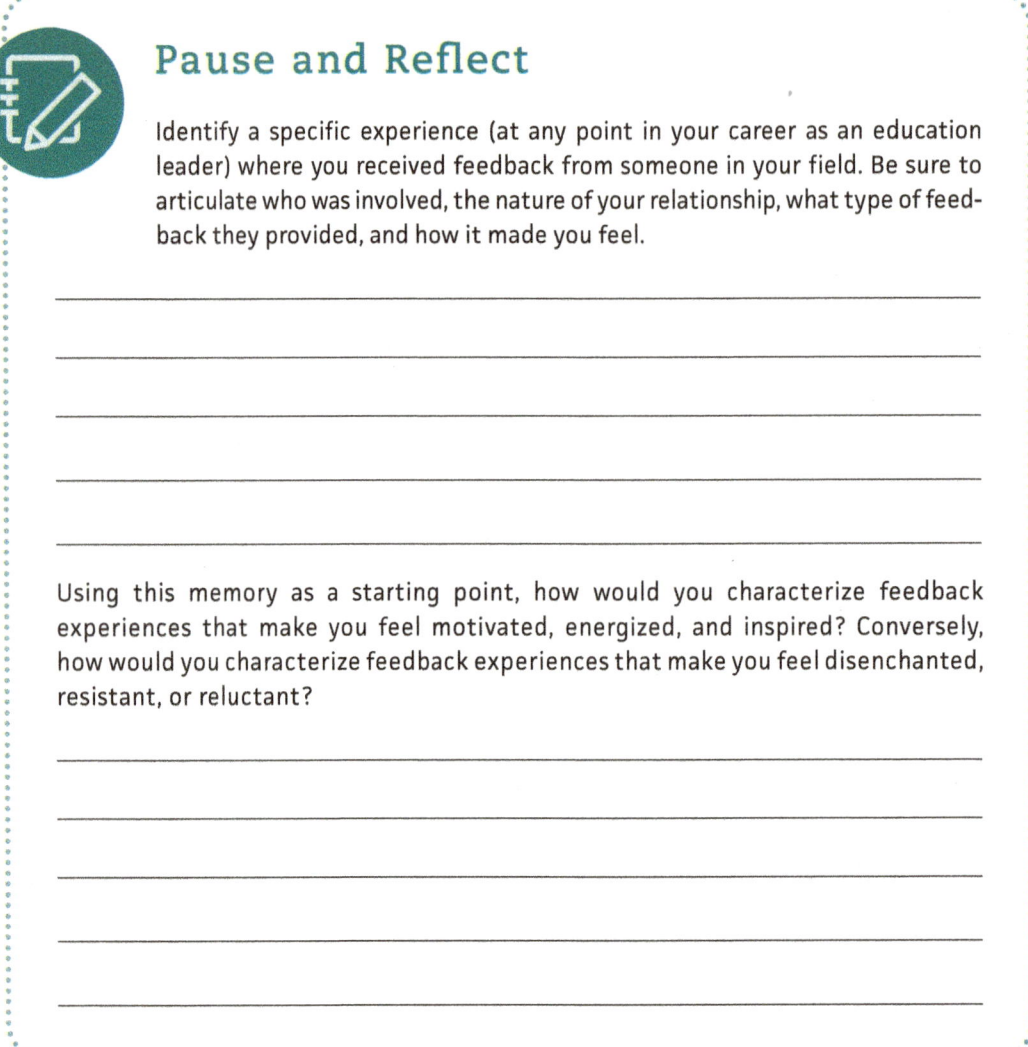

Pause and Reflect

Identify a specific experience (at any point in your career as an education leader) where you received feedback from someone in your field. Be sure to articulate who was involved, the nature of your relationship, what type of feedback they provided, and how it made you feel.

_____

_____

_____

_____

_____

Using this memory as a starting point, how would you characterize feedback experiences that make you feel motivated, energized, and inspired? Conversely, how would you characterize feedback experiences that make you feel disenchanted, resistant, or reluctant?

_____

_____

_____

_____

_____

You will have an opportunity to return to this reflection again soon. Let's now begin with Figure 8.2, to explore a variety of different mindsets that individuals may hold around the notion of seeking and/or receiving feedback.

FIGURE 8.2 ● Understanding Mindsets

FEEDBACK MINDSET	THIS MINDSET IS EXEMPLIFIED BY...	THIS MINDSET PUTS LEADERS AT RISK FOR...
GROWTH MINDSET		
Leaders with growth mindset view feedback as a valuable tool for personal and professional development.	Actively seeking feedback to improve their leadership, decision-making, and effectiveness in fostering a positive learning environment	Becoming overwhelmed or *stuck*, by competing input from varying sources of feedback Becoming dependent on feedback as the only source of guidance enabling you to make decisions or changes
FIXED MINDSET		
Leaders with a fixed mindset may believe that their abilities are static and that they either have the skills necessary to lead or they don't. These leaders may be more resistant to seeking or accepting feedback, viewing it as criticism or a threat to their competence.	The absence of seeking feedback in any instance Listening to or receiving feedback in any form and making no changes as a result of the information	Avoiding seeking feedback for fear of being seen as ineffective. Deflecting or minimizing constructive criticism
COLLABORATIVE MINDSET		
Leaders with collaborative mindset view feedback as a means of fostering a collective effort toward improving educational outcomes. They believe in shared leadership and encourage open, two-way communication between staff, students, and parents.	Actively seeking feedback from all stakeholders (teachers, students, parents) to make informed decisions Creating structures for regular, formal feedback (e.g., surveys, open forums) Valuing diverse perspectives and integrating feedback into strategic planning	Similar to Growth Mindset orientation, leaders may be at risk for becoming *data rich and information poor* if the focus is too strongly grounded in gathering the feedback and not sufficiently oriented in acting upon the feedback.
SERVANT LEADERSHIP MINDSET		
Education leaders with a servant leadership mindset prioritize the needs of their staff and students above their own. For them, feedback is critical because it helps them better serve their community.	Seeking feedback to understand how you can better support teachers and students Focusing on removing barriers to success based on the feedback you receive Empowering others by acting on the input you gather	If the focus shifts too significantly toward always meeting the needs of every stakeholder, decision-paralysis may ensue as a result of opposing viewpoints preventing a clear path forward.

(Continued)

(Continued)

FEEDBACK MINDSET	THIS MINDSET IS EXEMPLIFIED BY...	THIS MINDSET PUTS LEADERS AT RISK FOR...
ACCOUNTABILITY-DRIVEN MINDSET		
In this mindset, education leaders view feedback as essential for ensuring accountability and high standards.	Seeking data-driven feedback to track progress and performance metrics Using feedback to hold yourself and others accountable for outcomes Creating systems of feedback where teachers and staff are regularly evaluated to ensure alignment with school or district goals	Excessive attention to quantitative outcome metrics may disguise the equally important need for human-centered practices that ensure collective efficacy is generated in conjunction with the metrics.
RISK-AVERSE MINDSET		
Some leaders may fear that feedback will expose their weaknesses or challenge their authority. These leaders tend to avoid seeking feedback or only seek it selectively.	The absence of any feedback experiences Paying *lip service* to others who provide unsolicited feedback by listening and not making any subsequent changes	Being defensive or resistant when receiving negative feedback Seeking only positive or affirming feedback from trusted sources Avoiding feedback mechanisms that could reveal uncomfortable truths
REFLECTIVE MINDSET		
Leaders with a reflective mindset are introspective and constantly analyze their actions and decisions. Feedback is a tool for self-reflection, allowing them to gauge the impact of their leadership. Regularly seeking feedback is a way to reflect on their practices.	Taking time to process feedback and make meaningful changes based on it Encouraging reflection across the organization as part of a feedback culture	Over analysis of prior actions or decisions may consume time otherwise needed to equally focus on anticipating and planning for the future. This mindset may be driven by a need for validation from others and cause uncertainty amongst stakeholders.
FEARLESS MINDSET		
Leaders with a fearless mindset are not afraid of hearing difficult truths. They view all feedback, positive or constructive, as an opportunity to challenge the status quo and push for improvement.	Seeking candid, even critical, feedback without fear of judgment Encouraging staff to speak openly about challenges, bottlenecks, or flaws Being comfortable with vulnerability in leadership, as they believe it leads to authentic growth	This mindset requires fidelity to aligning words and actions. Leaders who insist on candid feedback from stakeholders, particularly those whom they supervise, cannot breach trust with negative or punitive reactions.

FEEDBACK MINDSET	THIS MINDSET IS EXEMPLIFIED BY . . .	THIS MINDSET PUTS LEADERS AT RISK FOR . . .
HIERARCHICAL MINDSET		
Some leaders may adopt a hierarchical mindset where feedback is seen as a one-way street. These leaders often view feedback as something that flows from the top down rather than seeking it from below.	Routinely providing unsolicited feedback to others and perhaps behaving dismissively when the feedback is reciprocated. Leaders are less likely to listen well to others without feeling compelled to offer advice or direction in response.	Rarely seeking feedback from subordinates, preferring to rely on your own experience and judgment Focusing on giving feedback to others rather than receiving it yourself Seeing feedback mechanisms as tools to enforce compliance rather than avenues for growth

Pause and Reflect

Return to the reflection you completed prior to examining the different mindsets. Based on your answers, which of these mindsets most closely aligns with how you typically approach feedback? What areas of any of these mindsets might be an approach you aspire to further develop?

_____

_____

_____

_____

_____

DEVELOPING YOUR FEEDBACK SOURCES

When developing your habits of seeking feedback to amplify your growth, knowing from whom to seek that feedback is a critical, early step. For example, there is little merit in asking for feedback from those you recognize are unlikely to be candid and honest. Author Scott (2019) of _Radical Candor_ calls this extremely passive feedback "ruinous empathy," a feedback approach that has little effect and can even be harmful by leading you to believe you are in need of no changes or adjustments. Conversely, Scott describes excessively aggressive feedback as "obnoxious aggression" when others do not have your well-being in mind and seek only to criticize without concern for your ultimate growth and impact. The most effective feedback sources balance care and directness, enabling you to hear delicate truths about where you may improve because they care deeply about you and believe in your capacity to improve. Using these criteria as a starting point, consider the different sources of feedback available to you as an education leader and ways in which you might engage them in your personal growth journey:

> **Teachers and Staff:** Feedback from teachers and staff is critical for understanding how leadership decisions affect the day-to-day operations of the school and the classroom environment. It helps leaders gauge how their strategies and initiatives are working on the ground and how well they are supporting staff. Teachers and staff can offer practical insights into what is helping or hindering classroom instruction, staff morale, and professional growth. You may find rich conversation opportunities with instructional staff who are *living out* the initiatives being implemented by your team and seek their feedback on operational effectiveness, policy implementation, professional development needs, and leadership communication. This is an example of an excellent data source such as those you explored in Chapter 7 and one that presents invaluable opportunity to amplify your habit of leading the learning in your school as described in Chapter 5!

> **Students:** Students may be most often excluded from the opportunity to provide you with feedback, and yet they are the group most impacted by the vast majority of your decisions! Student feedback can help provide another dimension or perspective as you evaluate the effectiveness of teaching methods, curriculum, and policies in how they foster an inclusive, engaging, and supportive learning environment. Finding opportunities to seek student input on their authentic learning experiences, classroom engagement, the school's culture, and overall student well-being can present rich and meaningful data for your team of adults to examine and for you to internalize as you seek your own growth.

> **Parents and Families:** While not immersed in the daily experiences of everyday school life, parents and families offer important insights into how the school is perceived

from the outside, how well the school communicates with the broader community, and how policies impact students beyond the classroom. Feedback from families helps leaders understand the effectiveness of home-school partnerships, the clarity of school communications, and how well the school supports student development holistically. Creating thoughtful, explicit opportunities for families to engage in providing feedback to the school merits identifying beforehand what types of feedback you might expect to receive and how you might act upon the information. Developing a trusting, open line of communication with families offers an exciting change to synergize efforts toward achieving the school's vision, particularly when leading change.

Supervisors: There may be patterns of thinking that you hold around seeking feedback from a supervisor that cause you to resist proactively pursuing such opportunities. Power dynamics can feel threatening at worst, or uncomfortable at minimum, and it's not unusual to avoid the risk of being seen as incompetent. Conversely, seeking feedback from your supervisors in a meaningful and specific way is far more likely to convey that you believe in the value of lifelong learning and view your role squarely as a lead learner of your school or district. Supervisors can provide you with a broader organizational and policy-level perspective and empower you with explicit feedback around how to engage in a way that helps you understand how well your school aligns with districtwide goals, policies, and expectations.

Professional Learning Networks: Networking with other education leaders through professional organizations, conferences, or online communities can provide you with a valuable sounding board on best practices, innovative strategies, and leadership challenges. For example, engaging with peers in similar roles can provide you with diverse perspectives, feedback on their practices, and opportunities to exchange ideas on overcoming common challenges.

Mentors and Coaches: While not always a realistic opportunity for every leader, the opportunity to work with a mentor or coach may be one of the most powerful feedback experiences of all. Serving as a thought partner who places your interests and needs as the highest priority, an experienced mentor or leadership coach can provide personalized, expert feedback on your development and decision-making.

The most effective feedback sources balance care and directness, enabling you to hear delicate truths about where you may improve because they care deeply about you and believe in your capacity to improve.

Pause and Reflect

How do you currently seek feedback from any of these groups? What new ways might you endeavor to become more intentional about seeking feedback from one of these groups you believe offers a significant opportunity to support your growth?

_____

_____

_____

_____

_____

APPLYING FEEDBACK FOR UTMOST IMPACT

When seeking feedback, not all the ideas and perspectives you gather will merit adopting or applying. A healthy filter will guide you to prioritize your decisions to respond to differing degrees, though always with a clear understanding of how the feedback serves the goals you are striving to attain. When it's time to take action, consider the strategies we also describe for educators in our book *Habits of Resilient Educators* (Prendergast & Lee, 2024).

1. **Synthesize the Information.** Gather the feedback in a structured manner that allows you to review and analyze the information easily. Look for themes as if you were on outside observer striving to garner the most salient points from the data to share back with others. From these themes, apply another layer of organizing based on your goals for seeking the feedback. Were you gathering information that might be immediately actionable?

Compare your themes against your current calendar and projects to identify exactly where you have time and bandwidth to engage. Or perhaps the feedback was reflective on past efforts, and you hope to refine a practice or strategy for the future. As you endeavor to improve the outcome of family engagement experiences, for example, the feedback from prior events can be distilled and used as a key component of planning efforts for the next one.

2. **Reflect on the Feedback Provided.** As a leader, you may find some sources of feedback are at risk for being less candid and honest as a result of power dynamics between you and the feedback provider (students or teachers, for example). Alternatively, there may be trends amongst the participants in a group who provided you feedback that merit acknowledgment as being driven by bias or personal agendas. In any instance, it is important to examine who provided the feedback. Who was provided a chance to give feedback and did not (by choice or accident, it's also important to discern)? Just like the habit of using data as an evaluative thinker in Chapter 7, where might you have *feedback deserts* across your stakeholders or at varying times of the year? Why might these patterns exist? How will you address any gaps in the feedback in the future in how you apply it or ways you gather it again?

3. **Choose What and How to Apply!** With an enhanced understanding of the nature of the feedback you gathered and what interpretations you have developed from it, it's time to look outward and determine the best plan to put it to work. Consider the merit of working with an accountability partner—someone close to you who will offer gentle support to encourage your efforts when your attention lags, for example. Communicate with the stakeholders who were involved in providing you with the feedback about your intentions and you may reap even more rewards with a supportive network! Acknowledging that you found value in their ideas and, perhaps more importantly, are intentionally applying them will serve to deepen the message for everyone that evaluative thinking is fundamental to the community's success as a whole. And finally, build in opportunities to celebrate your progress!

Where might you have feedback deserts across your stakeholders or at varying times of the year? Why might these patterns exist? How will you address any gaps in the feedback in the future in how you apply it or ways you gather it again?

FEEDBACK TO AMPLIFY
ALL RESILIENT LEADER HABITS

The habit of seeking feedback is applicable throughout this entire book, though it is situated toward the later chapters as an opportunity to now highlight specifically the unique ways in which feedback may amplify your growth and learning across each of the different habits. Throughout the book, for example, you've explored the concept of evaluative thinking (Hattie, 2023). Feedback may constitute a form of evidence and is an explicit practice of evaluative thinkers who seek to deeply understand the impact of their efforts in any arena. Notice the opportunities suggested in Figure 8.3 for applying feedback to each habit and take the opportunity to document your own ideas for even further growth. As an additional challenge, identify an accountability partner to join you in this journey and develop an action plan for practicing these new opportunities!

FIGURE 8.3 ● Feedback Examples for Different Habits

HABIT	OPPORTUNITIES TO SEEK FEEDBACK FOR THIS HABIT	MY OWN IDEAS FOR FEEDBACK TO SEEK AROUND THIS HABIT
Building boundaries, not walls	Sharing challenging scenarios with a mentor or coach where you may be at risk for overextending yourself can be an opportunity for feedback on the behavior patterns you demonstrate with others that lead to diminished boundaries and ideas for how to adjust your actions.	
Filling your own bucket first	Notice a colleague or member of your staff who seems to "have it all together" and models a well-balanced life? Consider sharing an example with this individual of when you have felt drained and unmotivated. Gather their input on what they might do if they found themselves in this situation to prioritize their personal well-being.	
Casting a vision	Within the chapter on the habit of casting a vision, you engaged in an experience around zeroing in on your broader purpose as a leader. Identify an individual you consider a highly trusted thought partner who knows you quite well, if possible. Invite them to provide you feedback around what they perceive your purpose as an education leader to be, encouraging them to provide specific examples where possible.	

HABIT	OPPORTUNITIES TO SEEK FEEDBACK FOR THIS HABIT	MY OWN IDEAS FOR FEEDBACK TO SEEK AROUND THIS HABIT
	This feedback provides excellent content to compare against what you documented in the activity and see where they align or where there may be areas to become more intentional!	
Checking your blind spots	Let your staff know you are aiming to improve your understanding of how a particular initiative, project, etc., is being experienced. Create a brief survey to gather anonymous input and you are likely to identify a blind spot (or several!) about the difference between how you thought it was going and how others see it occurring. Most importantly, share your noticings and be sure to convey how you will change your approach!	
Leading as a learner	As a lead learner, one of the most principal activities you may engage in is that of observing classroom instruction where, as discussed in Chapter 5, you are at risk for the influence of unconscious bias. Invite feedback from teachers using an anonymous survey with questions such as "I know what my supervisor is looking for when observing instruction," or "My supervisor treats all teachers fairly when conducting observations and providing feedback." As with the feedback on your blind spots, be certain you share a synopsis of your new understandings from the survey and how you intend to make shifts!	
Upholding high expectations for all	This habit presents an opportunity to seek feedback from a very close friend, colleague, or family member (or several). Pose the question (in writing or in person): "In a scenario when someone I have asked to do something fails to deliver on my expectation, how do I most commonly respond?" This deceptively simple question will likely reveal your unacknowledged behavior patterns that affirm how you think you uphold expectations of others is actually how you do uphold expectations of others.	

(Continued)

(Continued)

HABIT	OPPORTUNITIES TO SEEK FEEDBACK FOR THIS HABIT	MY OWN IDEAS FOR FEEDBACK TO SEEK AROUND THIS HABIT
Data habits of evaluative thinkers	Leaders may often be at risk for becoming awash in enormous amounts of data and failing to share the data effectively, act upon the data in a meaningful way, or help their team to understand the data. Consider starting with a group of teachers—those most likely to interact with data alongside you—and invite them to describe as many examples as possible of when they recall you taking specific action as a result of student learning data. Depending on the range of responses (or lack thereof), you will gain a broad understanding of whether the actions you believe you have taken are visibly apparent to the practitioners in your school.	

The Big Ideas

From leading the learning, to refining your data use skills, and now the art of gathering and leveraging feedback to elevate your impact across areas of your work, you are well on your way down the path to connecting each of the habits of resilient educators to amplify their influence on your leadership. The habit of getting and using feedback is tactfully positioned at this later phase of the book to illuminate its merit as a tool for using with every single other habit. As you learned in this chapter how feedback is always all around us, whether solicited or not, you should now recognize the opportunity that you have to be highly intentional and tactical about selecting what feedback to gather and how to use it for utmost benefit. In turn, you will become a model of the *lead learner* in your system as you strive to cultivate a mindset of continuous improvement in others and articulate how this looks in practice when you constantly seek feedback from others to grow and progress.

Just as you examined practices and processes to know the impact of your decisions, initiatives, ideas, and more, now you have practices and processes to know your own impact.

Let's Reflect

1. Prior to reading this chapter, how would you characterize your attitude toward seeking feedback for yourself? How has your mindset toward feedback shifted because of the ideas around this habit?

   _____

   _____

   _____

2. What will be your immediate next step to apply the new learning from this chapter to your efforts at growth across the other habits you have studied thus far?

   _____

   _____

   _____

3. What challenges do you envision encountering as you delve into the habit of seeking and using feedback from many sources? What actions will you take to mitigate the effect of these challenges?

   _____

   _____

   _____

What's Next?

In the next chapter, "Don't Travel Alone," you will explore the vital role that the habit of developing a strong professional network plays in the success of educational leaders. A thriving network isn't just about exchanging business cards; it's about building authentic, supportive relationships with colleagues, mentors, and other professionals who can offer fresh perspectives, resources, and collaboration opportunities. You'll examine strategies for cultivating meaningful connections and learn how a robust network can help you navigate challenges, stay informed on best practices, and foster personal and professional growth. By investing in your network, you're not only advancing your career but also enhancing your ability to serve your school community more effectively.

CHAPTER 9

Don't Travel Alone

Dr. Penz, a dedicated elementary principal in his eighteenth year, consistently faced challenges in building connections with other educational leaders. Due to serving in a relatively isolated district, Penz found it challenging to find established networks or professional communities. Furthermore, Penz, like many leaders, harbored concerns about appearing vulnerable or in need of support. These beliefs created resistance to the idea of seeking collaboration for professional growth. Yet Penz recognized the importance of overcoming these barriers in order to enhance his leadership capacity and support his school and district growth. He began by reevaluating his time management strategies, carving out dedicated periods for networking, and leveraging virtual platforms to connect with educational leaders beyond his immediate geographic area. Additionally, Penz took proactive steps to seek out online networks and communities that aligned with his professional goals and values. Through these virtual communities, he started engaging in discussions, sharing experiences, and seeking advice from peers, thereby transcending the limitations of his district's physical isolation. Penz identified influential mentor figures within these online networks, realizing that seeking guidance and collaborating with others did not diminish his expertise, but rather enriched it. Once Penz experienced the tangible benefits of collaboration, he worked to dispel myths about the downsides of connecting with other leaders within his district, too. By openly sharing the positive outcomes of his collaborative efforts and fostering a culture of mutual support within his own school and district, he demonstrated the value of collective professional growth and challenged the misconceptions that had previously hindered his networking efforts. Ultimately, by acknowledging and addressing the barriers that impeded his ability to connect with others, Penz not only enhanced his professional growth and leadership skills but also inspired a culture of open collaboration and networking within his school and district, leading to improved outcomes for students and the broader educational community.

WHY COLLABORATION, NETWORKING, AND THINKING PARTNERSHIPS MATTER

In the realm of education leadership, the ability to seek external guidance, share ideas, and find emotional support plays a crucial role in fostering success and growth. By developing the habit of looking outside oneself for answers to questions, ideas for solving challenges, and support for shouldering the emotions leaders experience, education professionals can recognize the immense merit of approaching their work as a community or network, as opposed to an isolated endeavor. Leaders need strategies for determining the type of networks that serve individual needs, how to build them, and the practices for intentionally leveraging their value to foster continuous growth as an education leader.

> *By developing the habit of looking outside oneself for answers to questions, ideas for solving challenges, and support for shouldering the emotions leaders experience, education professionals can recognize the immense merit of approaching their work as a community or network, as opposed to an isolated endeavor.*

Thus, as education leaders, we should assess specific needs and aspirations to identify the type of networks that would serve us best. This involves reflecting on strengths and areas for growth, as well as acknowledging the challenges we encounter within our leadership roles. For instance, if you are struggling with technology integration, you might seek out a network of educators and professionals with expertise in this area. Similarly, if you are facing challenges in creating an inclusive and diverse school culture, you might seek a network focused on equity and diversity in education. By understanding your own unique needs, you can make informed decisions about the kind of networks that can offer the most relevant support and resources. Many professional leaders leverage needs and skills assessments, as well as seek input from experts outside their field of expertise to enrich their learning experiences. For example, when a leader finds themselves grappling with complex personal challenges, tapping into the insights of a specialist in social and emotional expertise can prove invaluable. Embracing external support beyond traditional education experts not only offers a fresh viewpoint but is also gaining traction as a welcomed practice within educational environments. As we discussed in Chapter 5, leaders need to be seen as learners, and there is a clear connection between the habit of lead learner and the habit of not traveling alone. Therefore, finding your own networks, mentors, and thought partners supports both habits. When leaders model learning and have their own networks and mentors, educators view them as putting their words into action. This could involve joining professional organizations, attending conferences and workshops, or participating in online communities and forums. Engaging with colleagues and peers through social media platforms, virtual meetings, or local networking events can also play a significant role in expanding one's network. Research shows that "principals' leadership practices are key in promoting teacher collaboration, cultivating collective participation and responsibility among staff, building trust, improving organizational culture, and encouraging research-based and collaborative learning practices within schools" (Sahlin, 2022, p. 48).

Once you have identified the networks you want to be a part of, then you can start building and fostering those connections. Be patient when making connections with these networks as this takes time and that is something we know brings forth its own challenges. Prioritizing these networks and connections will pay off down the road. Establishing meaningful and authentic connections is essential, allowing leaders to build relationships based on trust, mutual respect, and a genuine exchange of ideas and experiences (see Figure 9.1).

FIGURE 9.1 ● Characteristics of Building a Meaningful Network

BUILDING A MEANINGFUL NETWORK IS....	BUILDING A MEANINGFUL NETWORK IS NOT...
Initiating, cultivating, and maintaining a range of professional relationships	Limiting your network to only those who think like you and share your areas of expertise
Sharing resources and tips with your network, and gaining new ideas relevant to your work to implement in your setting	Only receiving expertise and ideas from others without reciprocating or offering your support to others
Leveraging creative and critical thinking partnerships to develop your own leadership practice	Adopting a myopic view of your work as a leader or resisting opportunities to growth by believing others have little to offer you
Providing mutual support across your network by lifting others' voices, celebrating others' achievements, and giving and receiving support when faced with challenges	Using your colleagues to publicize your successes and achievements without reciprocating and supporting others' success without genuine admiration

As a leader, you should keep an open mind and be proactive in seeking out connections and opportunities. By identifying and engaging with networks, mentors, and thought partners, leaders can gain new insights, knowledge, and perspectives, fostering their own personal and professional development.

Pause and Reflect

Use the reflective questions to help you identify ways you may want to learn and grow as a leader and guide you in setting goals and seeking out the type of support you may need or desire.

What specific areas of my leadership practice do I want to improve?

_____

_____

_____

_____

_____

What are my long-term career goals, and how can a mentor or thought partner support me in achieving them?

_____

_____

_____

_____

_____

What type of mentorship do I need—someone with experience in a specific area, leadership style, or organizational context?

_____

_____

_____

_____

_____

How do I learn best, and what would align with my learning preferences?

_____

_____

_____

_____

_____

What challenges or opportunities am I currently facing that could benefit from mentorship or thought partner guidance?

_____

_____

_____

_____

_____

What resources or support systems do I currently have in place and what do I need?

_____

_____

_____

_____

_____

LEADERS DON'T LET THEIR STAFF TRAVEL ALONE

Leaders play an integral role in building a positive school culture that values teamwork and collective learning efforts. Developing a collaborative school culture is essential for fostering engagement, innovation, and overall student success. As a leader, there are several vital qualities that need to be cultivated to establish and maintain a collaborative environment within a school. The qualities that nurture a culture of collaboration are as follows:

- trust
- effective communication
- empathy and emotional intelligence
- shared vision
- conflict resolution
- flexibility and adaptability

Experience and research remind us that trust is crucial in school culture between colleagues and administration. When educators are comfortable sharing ideas and working together to solve challenges, it is evident there is a culture of trust within the teammates. This collaborative approach leads to more creative problem-solving that benefits students. Trust and reliance forms the foundation of strong relationships in education, which can be achieved by building faith with the entire school community. As a leader, being open and honest in decision-making is important. By building faith with teachers, students, and parents, you can create a transparent environment where everyone feels included and informed. Furthermore, transparency is essential for fostering trust within the school community. Leaders and educators should always practice honesty and integrity in their actions, as transparency is rooted in reliability, and reliability is rooted in trust. It is important to communicate truthfully and maintain credibility to build trust within the community. While it may be challenging to speak uncomfortable truths that can evoke emotional reactions, being patient with yourself and prioritizing transparency will ultimately foster trust among your staff and students.

While it may be challenging to speak uncomfortable truths that can evoke emotional reactions, being patient with yourself and prioritizing transparency will ultimately foster trust among your staff and students.

Pause and Reflect

Use these reflective questions to think about how trust impacts collaboration:

Reflect on a leader that you have respected in your professional career. What did that leader do to build trust with you? Did that leader have a trusting relationship with others on your team?

_____

_____

_____

_____

_____

What percentage of staff in your building or department currently trust you? What do you think is contributing to this? What do you want to do to increase trust with you and with your school environment?

_____

_____

_____

_____

_____

Do you think students and families are trusting your educators? What do you need to celebrate? What do you need to support?

_____

_____

_____

_____

_____

You may want to dive deeper into trust if you are seeing this as an area that your team needs to grow or chooses to focus on. The trust matrix provided in Figure 9.2 allows you to assess team performance in each dimension to identify areas for improvement and strengthen trust within the school community. By prioritizing these dimensions and consistently demonstrating trustworthiness, you can build a culture of trust that fosters collaboration, engagement, and positive relationships within the school environment.

FIGURE 9.2 ● Trust Matrix for School Leaders

TRUST DIMENSION	DESCRIPTION	EXAMPLES
Transparency	Openness and honesty in communication	Sharing information openly with all stakeholders Explaining decision-making processes clearly
Integrity	Demonstrating honesty and ethical behavior	Consistently following through on promises Maintaining confidentiality when required
Competence	Demonstrating knowledge and skills	Making informed decisions based on data and best practices Seeking professional development to improve skills
Empathy	Showing care and understanding for others	Listening actively to the concerns of staff, students, and parents Addressing individual needs with sensitivity
Consistency	Acting predictably and reliably	Following through on commitments Remaining consistent in behavior and decision-making

FOSTERING EMOTIONAL REGULATION WITHIN ADULTS

In educational settings, fostering emotional regulation among adults, including teachers, administrators, and staff, is paramount for creating a supportive and effective learning environment. Adults who can regulate their emotions are better equipped to model healthy emotional behaviors for students, handle conflict constructively, and provide an emotionally safe space for learning and growth. By nurturing emotional regulation skills in adults through training, self-care practices, and ongoing support, educational institutions can cultivate a culture of empathy, resilience, and effective communication and collaboration. When leaders commit to focusing on their own emotional regulations, the immediate outcome is a positive environment that benefits the entire school community.

However, like many professions, our undergraduate and graduate education programs focus on how to teach, and what to teach, but do not prepare our educators for the complex stressors they encounter daily that require strategies to help emotionally regulate throughout the day. One strategy or concept that can help foster collaboration, empathy, and resilience is called the "window of tolerance." The window of tolerance, initially introduced by Dr. Dan Siegel, refers to the optimal state of arousal in which an individual can effectively process and respond to stressors without becoming overwhelmed or dysregulated. This state enables individuals to engage in learning, problem-solving, and social interactions constructively. When individuals operate within their window of tolerance, they can regulate their emotions, maintain focus, and exhibit adaptive coping strategies. However, when arousal levels exceed this window, individuals may experience hyperarousal, characterized by heightened stress and reactivity, or hypoarousal, marked by disengagement and withdrawal.

By drawing on insights from neuroscience and psychology, we can explore how the window of tolerance framework can inform educational leaders in creating supportive, inclusive, and emotionally regulated educational environments. The concept of the "window of tolerance" provides a valuable framework for understanding the optimal range of arousal within which individuals can effectively process and respond to stimuli. In the context of education leadership, the application of this concept holds great promise in creating environments that support emotional regulation, inclusion, and ultimately resiliency. When individuals are bumped out of their window of tolerance, they may not feel psychologically safe, and this may cause a trauma response. The trauma response for individuals shows up in several different ways. Some individuals may seem combative as their trauma response is to fight, while other individuals may withdraw because their natural trauma response is flight, flee, or fawn. These responses, deeply rooted in our survival instincts, show up in team meetings, the staff lounge, and frequently administrators' offices. Often leaders and educators recognize these responses in students and parents, but not their peers. It is essential to remember that the human experience no matter what age, when faced with perceived threats or danger, individuals may exhibit one of these responses as part of their survival mechanism. These individuals have been bumped out of their "window of tolerance."

Pause and Reflect

Have You Ever Experienced a Terrible Meeting or Toxic Team?

What do you remember about that experience?

PHYSICAL EXPERIENCE
What do you remember physically? Example: your body was tense, breathing got harder, neck or face got blotchy, clench your jaw?

EMOTIONAL EXPERIENCE
What do you remember emotionally? Example: angry, hurt, sad, mad, disengaged?

MENTAL EXPERIENCE
What do you remember mentally? Example: unable to collaborate, unable to be creative, or unable to think deeply and clearly?

Have You Experienced a Highly Effective Team, Thinking Partner, or Meeting?

What do you remember about that experience?

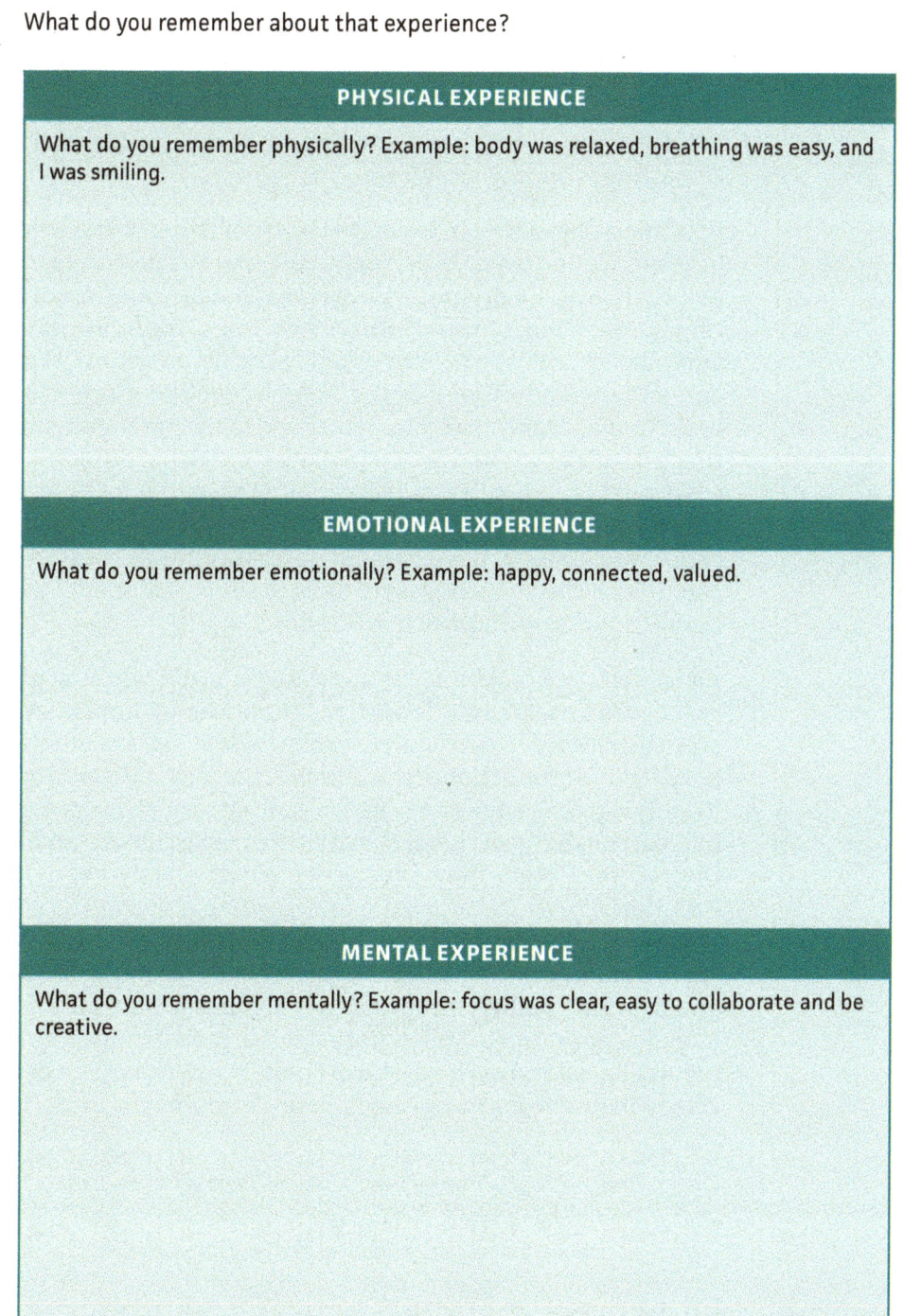

PHYSICAL EXPERIENCE

What do you remember physically? Example: body was relaxed, breathing was easy, and I was smiling.

EMOTIONAL EXPERIENCE

What do you remember emotionally? Example: happy, connected, valued.

MENTAL EXPERIENCE

What do you remember mentally? Example: focus was clear, easy to collaborate and be creative.

It is essential to understand these trauma responses to better recognize and regulate our emotional reactions in challenging circumstances. Equally important is the opportunity to reflect on the experiences or environments that we were psychologically safe in, often described by characteristics that promote collaboration, trust, creativity, empowerment, confidence, and competence. Inviting your staff, colleagues, thought partners, and/or mentors to reflect on what helps them remain in their window of tolerance and the positive outcome of that is a terrific grounding activity.

Educational leaders can leverage the framework of the window of tolerance to create emotionally safe and supportive learning environments. By promoting practices that facilitate emotional regulation, such as mindfulness exercises, trauma-informed approaches, and social-emotional learning programs, leaders can enhance adult well-being, which leads to student well-being and academic success. Moreover, fostering a staff culture that acknowledges and accommodates individual differences in emotional processing and regulation is essential for creating a conducive learning environment. Educational leaders can prioritize professional development opportunities that equip educators with the knowledge and tools to support students within their respective windows of tolerance.

As leaders and learners, we can integrate the window of tolerance framework into leadership practices by implementing strategies that recognize and accommodate diverse emotional needs within the school community. This may involve creating flexible learning environments, promoting restorative practices, and establishing supportive structures for students and staff to seek help when they experience emotional dysregulation. Additionally, as leaders we can prioritize a strengths-based approach to education, focusing on adults' and students' resilience and strengths rather than solely addressing challenges and deficits. Finally, by promoting a compassionate and understanding approach to collaboration while prioritizing emotional regulation, education leaders can create an environment conducive to inclusive learning and holistic development.

Leaders can prioritize a strengths-based approach to education, focusing on adults' and students' resilience and strengths rather than solely addressing challenges and deficits.

The Big Ideas

In this chapter, we outlined the challenges a school principal or leader has in building connections with other educational leaders. We reflected on the importance of overcoming barriers to networking and collaboration, particularly in isolated or resource-limited settings, and highlighted the benefits of seeking support and guidance from peers and mentors. Furthermore, we emphasized the significance of seeking external guidance, sharing ideas, and finding emotional support as essential components of education leadership. We reflected on how to effectively seek out networks, mentors, and thought partners to gain new insights, knowledge, and perspectives, fostering personal and professional development. Next, we delved into the significant role trust plays in building a collaborative school culture. When reflecting on resilience, we provided strategies that support effective communication, showing empathy, maintaining consistency, and fostering emotional regulation among staff. Finally, we introduced and reflected on the concept of the "window of tolerance" as a framework for understanding emotional regulation and resilience. This chapter emphasizes the alignment of this concept with educational leadership and its potential in creating emotionally regulated, inclusive, and supportive learning environments.

Let's Reflect

1. How have my own emotional responses influenced the school culture and collaboration within my educational setting? In what ways can I improve my emotional regulation to better support my staff and students?

   _____

   _____

   _____

2. What steps can I take to enhance trust and build a more collaborative environment within my school community? How can I demonstrate empathy, consistency, and effective communication to create a culture of trust and support?

   _____

   _____

   _____

   (Continued)

(Continued)

3. Reflecting on my professional growth and long-term career goals, what type of mentorship and learning partnerships do I need to further develop in my educational leadership journey? How can I actively seek out and engage with networks, mentors, and thought partners to support my ongoing development and leadership effectiveness?

_____

_____

_____

What's Next

You are now approaching the final habit of the book, Managing Change. While each of the habits uniquely influences your abilities to lead change in a school or district, this habit has been positioned as a culmination of the book as a manner of drawing on the various practices and approaches you have studied in preparation to master the art of change leadership. In a contemporary era of volatility, uncertainty, change, and anxiety (VUCA) across the education landscape, change leadership may be one of the most crucial skillsets to develop of the century. This final habit will synthesize your recent learning on the habits and prepare you for sustaining your utmost resilience as a leader in the face of any environment and any circumstance.

CHAPTER 10

Manage Change, or It Will Manage You

The Habits of a Resilient Leader

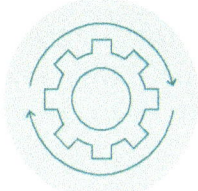

Lucas, a fourth-year principal in an elementary school with several different leadership experiences in other districts, was excited to finally find himself at the helm of a highly regarded school with a long history of implementing the practice of standards-based grading (SBG). As a passionate advocate of SBG himself, Lucas had heard of the strong reputation of this school and found himself puzzled why the entire team of previous administrators had left the school at once. Over the course of many meetings with teachers, families, and students in the first months of the year, however, Lucas was crestfallen to recognize what was disguised beneath the school's public reputation. The years of previous work to change the school completely away from traditional grading and full adoption of SBG were rife with complaint letters from stakeholders, significant staff turnover rates, and reports of the "disasters" that had resulted from administrators' efforts to implement mandatory compliance with policies. An entire group of teachers, in fact, told Lucas that they had never used the SBG policies and certainly wouldn't begin doing so now. Surprisingly, the Board of Directors was adamant that the SBG practices continue, naming them as a "flagship" of the school's reputation. In a series of conversations with his mentor, Lucas unpacked the very different leadership journey he knew was now ahead of him: he was tasked with beginning the change journey

toward implementing SBG from scratch. He would need to undo massive amounts of cynicism and resistance, lay the foundation for a new path forward, and compel authentic engagement if he hoped to have any success at all. Lucas had led change at small scales before, but the years ahead suddenly looked incredibly different than he had anticipated. He wondered to himself how he might survive this journey with his integrity intact. Resilience, without question, would be fundamental to his success.

WHY FOCUS ON THE HABIT OF LEADING CHANGE

Leading through change requires sophisticated emotional intelligence, of which resilience is a foundational component. Notice the suggestion in the title that, if you do not become adept at managing change, that change will *manage you*. The experiences of uncertainty, stress, and elevated demands around important and consequential decisions, for example, can have an enormously challenging impact on your well-being. As an education leader, you're often tasked with guiding change in a complex and evolving environment. The demands of managing teams, implementing new initiatives, and fostering a culture of growth require not only vision and strategy but a profound level of resilience. Developing the habit of cultivating resilience equips you to navigate the inevitable obstacles that come with leading transformation—whether that's resistance from stakeholders, the unpredictability of external factors, or the emotional toll of sustaining momentum over time.

Building and maintaining your resilience throughout change journeys isn't about avoiding challenges; it's about developing the capacity to bounce back from setbacks, learn from them, and continue to move forward with clarity and purpose. Resilience enables you to become more adaptable and able to sustain the energy and focus needed to inspire those around us. Resilient leaders show their teams that perseverance and flexibility are essential, not just in reaching short-term goals, but in creating long-lasting, meaningful change.

Resilience enables you to become more adaptable and able to sustain the energy and focus needed to inspire those around us.

A key aspect of resilience is understanding that setbacks are part of the process. As you explored in Chapter 8, you may often feel the pressure to have all the answers, but resilient leaders embrace vulnerability—acknowledging that uncertainty is a natural part of innovation. Building your skills as a lead learner, for example, in Chapter 5, means modeling resilience for your team. In doing so, you give your team permission to take risks, make mistakes, and learn from them, cultivating a culture where growth is a shared journey rather than a series of isolated successes.

By developing resilience, you also protect your own well-being. The emotional demands of leadership are significant, and without resilience, it's easy to become overwhelmed, leading to burnout or diminished effectiveness. Prioritizing your emotional strength and mental clarity not only serves you but empowers your ability to support and uplift those who depend on your guidance.

Resilience is the backbone of effective leadership, particularly in times of change. By committing to this habit, you'll foster a more positive, adaptive environment and lead with the steady, purposeful energy necessary to transform your vision into reality. We all face challenges in leadership, but by building resilience, we ensure that those challenges become stepping stones rather than stumbling blocks (see Figure 10.1).

FIGURE 10.1 ● Characteristics of Resilient Change Leadership

RESILIENT CHANGE LEADERSHIP IS . . .	RESILIENT CHANGE LEADERSHIP IS NOT . . .
Recognizing that you are empowered to control your outlook and seek hope and optimism for yourself and others no matter the circumstance	Believing that you are incapable of influencing your mindset or the mindset of others amidst times of change
Acknowledging that the challenges amidst a change are stressful and may be difficult while also modeling for your community that you are investing in your personal well-being so you may be of utmost service to their needs	Investing in superficial treatments (e.g., personal rewards such as shopping or food) and believing they will resolve your extreme feelings of stress and uncertainty
Demonstrating authentic communication skills amidst a change experience to foster confidence and a sense of agency in yourself and your community despite the presence of uncertainty and doubt	Communicating to your stakeholders that "everything is fine" to convey an image of control when in reality you are struggling to navigate the challenges of a change experience

RESILIENCE AND CHANGE LEADERSHIP: AN INSEPARABLE COMBINATION

Resilience in the context of education leadership refers to the capacity of school leaders to adapt, recover, and thrive in the face of challenges, pressures, and setbacks within your environment. Resilient leaders embody the ability to maintain a clear vision, take decisive actions, and sustain a positive mindset despite the various stressors and demands inherent in leading schools.

Leading change requires a combination of emotional intelligence, adaptability, and a focus on both people and systems. Critical to your success is the ability to recognize the power of mindset. Resilient leaders approach obstacles with hope and optimism, trusting that solutions can be found (Fernandez et al., 2020). By reframing challenges as opportunities for growth, for example, you set a tone of possibility, encouraging your team to rise to the occasion. Your outlook has a ripple effect, influencing the emotional climate of your school or organization.

As leaders, we often focus on supporting others, but developing resilience means recognizing that we, too, have control over how we respond to change. Researchers Southwick and Charney (2018) describe various specific factors that influence the ability of individuals to experience resilience. Among them are realistic optimism, brain fitness, meaning and purpose, and cognitive and emotional flexibility. As an education leader, you may apply these by taking ownership of your own development by seeking learning opportunities (as you examined in Chapter 5), whether through professional networks, mentorship, or reflective practice. Perhaps you consciously choose to engage in habits that strengthen your emotional and mental health, such as regular reflection, mindfulness, or setting aside time for self-care. Southwick and Charney assert that a specific mindset of resilience that enables you to experience confidence and control amidst times of change is to stay connected with your purpose (2018). In moments of upheaval, reconnecting with your core values and vision—just as you learned in Chapter 3—can provide much-needed clarity and stability. Purpose provides you an anchor, giving direction when change feels overwhelming. Aligning your purpose with the goals you set for your school or district allows you to lead with intention, ensuring that decisions, even difficult ones, are grounded in a bigger picture.

Pause and Reflect

Building upon these various factors that contribute to your resilience, use the chart to examine examples of change scenarios within a school setting and consider how a leader may model resilience while navigating them. In the empty spaces, practice developing your own ideas for how you might employ resilience in these settings.

CHANGE SCENARIO EXAMPLE: IMPLEMENTING A NEW CURRICULUM WITH STAFF RESISTANCE	
Resilience Factors That May Help: Cognitive flexibility, growth mindset	
Examples of Applying Resilience: Stay flexible and maintain open communication with staff, encouraging feedback and adaptation. Use setbacks as opportunities to adjust the approach while reinforcing the shared vision.	**My Ideas for Applying Resilience:**
CHANGE SCENARIO EXAMPLE: BUDGET CUTS IMPACTING STUDENT PROGRAMS	
Resilience Factors That May Help: Facing fear, realistic optimism, focus on vision	
Shift focus from the loss to finding innovative solutions. Engage the community in creative problem-solving and prioritize needs without losing sight of the school's mission.	**My Ideas for Applying Resilience:**
CHANGE SCENARIO EXAMPLE: LEADING A MAJOR SCHOOL MERGER OR REORGANIZATION	
Resilience Factors That May Help: Realistic optimism, focus on vision, engage social support	
Acknowledge the complexity of change and focus on long-term goals. Maintain patience, manage emotions, and steadily guide stakeholders through the uncertainties and stresses of the transition.	**My Ideas for Applying Resilience:**
CHANGE SCENARIO EXAMPLE: STUDENT PERFORMANCE NOT MEETING ESTABLISHED EXPECTATIONS	
Resilience Factors That May Help: Facing fear, realistic optimism, persistence in the face of setbacks, embracing cognitive flexibility	
Use resilience to avoid blame and instead focus on continuous improvement. Engage teachers, students, and families in a collaborative effort to assess strategies and implement gradual changes based on feedback.	**My Ideas for Applying Resilience:**

(Continued)

(Continued)

<table>
<tr><td colspan="2" align="center">**CHANGE SCENARIO EXAMPLE: HANDLING A SIGNIFICANT PUBLIC RELATIONS CRISIS**</td></tr>
<tr><td colspan="2">**Resilience Factors That May Help:** Engage social networks, focus on vision, facing fear</td></tr>
<tr><td>Stay calm under pressure, focus on clear and transparent communication, and use the opportunity to rebuild trust. Reflect on lessons learned to strengthen future crisis management plans.</td><td>**My Ideas for Applying Resilience:**</td></tr>
</table>

Where have you noticed you already possess personal strengths in the areas that define resilience? Where have you noticed areas that merit prioritization for your growth?

_____

_____

_____

_____

_____

STRATEGIES FOR BUILDING YOUR RESILIENCE TOOLBOX

As leaders in education, your ability to guide others through change and adversity begins with your own capacity to navigate challenges with strength and clarity. Resilience isn't a trait you either have or don't have; it's a skill you can cultivate over time. Several of the most essential components of building resilience are as follows:

- self-awareness
- emotional intelligence
- empathy for yourself and others
- a strong support network

By strengthening these areas, you not only enhance your own well-being but also become more effective leaders for your teams and communities. Here we will explore practical strategies to help you develop these areas further and build the personal resilience skills needed to thrive in your leadership role. We'll focus on key approaches to enhancing emotional intelligence, such as regulating emotions, empathizing with others, and maintaining composure in difficult situations. You'll also examine the role of self-awareness, which allows you to recognize our own emotional triggers, understand your leadership strengths and weaknesses, and make conscious choices that align with your values.

Resilience isn't a trait you either have or don't have; it's a skill you can cultivate over time.

DEVELOP SELF-AWARENESS

While leading schools and managing teams, it's easy to become absorbed in the external demands and forget to look inward. However, when we take the time to understand ourselves—our emotions, triggers, strengths, and blind spots—we become better equipped to make thoughtful decisions, respond more effectively to challenges, and ultimately lead in ways that align with our values. Here are some suggestions to support your development of self-awareness:

- **Reflect Regularly on Your Experiences:** As a leader, you are constantly in motion, moving from one issue to the next. However, making time for reflection is key to self-awareness. Consider setting aside a few moments at the end of each day or week to think about the situations you've faced. Ask yourself: *What went well? What didn't go as planned? How did I feel in those moments, and what might have triggered those emotions?* Journaling can also be an effective way to capture these reflections and notice patterns in your behavior and thought processes.

- **Employ Your Feedback-Seeking Habits:** It can be challenging to see ourselves as others see us. That's why it's important to seek input from those around us—whether that's your leadership team, peers, or even teachers and staff members. Embrace the strategies in Chapter 8 to multiply their impact on your self-awareness and, ultimately, your resilience.

- **Recognize and Explore Emotional Triggers:** We all have emotional triggers—situations or interactions that cause us to react impulsively or emotionally. These triggers are often deeply rooted and can be difficult to identify. When you find yourself feeling particularly frustrated, defensive, or anxious, pause and ask yourself these questions: *What about this situation is triggering me? Is this reaction more about me than the situation at hand?* Over time, recognizing your emotional triggers will allow you to take a step back when they arise and respond with greater control and empathy.

- **Revisit Your Purpose and Align Your Actions:** Dig even more deeply into the practices within the habit of being the vision caster (Chapter 3)! When you're faced with tough decisions, ask yourself these questions: *Is this choice consistent with my values? Does it reflect the kind of leader I want to be for my school and community?* Aligning your actions with your values will help you lead authentically and foster deeper trust with those you lead.

BUILD EMOTIONAL INTELLIGENCE

Cultivating emotional intelligence is essential for any education leader looking to build stronger relationships, navigate challenges with empathy, and foster a positive school culture. Emotional intelligence, at its core, is the ability to recognize, understand, and manage not only our own emotions but also those of others. As leaders, this skill allows us to respond thoughtfully to difficult situations, support our teams effectively, and lead with compassion, even in the face of adversity. Here are some suggestions to support your development of emotional intelligence:

- **Practice Active Listening:** You are likely often expected to provide solutions, but sometimes the most powerful thing you can do is simply listen. Active listening means being fully present in conversations, not just hearing the words, but understanding the emotions behind them. When someone on your team comes to you with a concern, resist the urge to immediately solve the problem. Instead, listen deeply, ask clarifying questions, and acknowledge their feelings. This not only helps you understand their perspective better but also shows your team that you value their input and emotions.

- **Manage Your Emotional Reactions:** One of the most important aspects of emotional intelligence is the ability to regulate your own emotions. Leading in education can be stressful, and there will inevitably be moments of frustration, disappointment, or overwhelm. When these emotions arise, it's important to take a step back before reacting. Practice pausing when you feel triggered—take a few deep breaths, give yourself a moment to collect your thoughts, and then respond in a way that reflects your values as a leader. This practice not only helps you maintain composure but also sets a calm and measured tone for those around you.

- **Recognize Emotional Patterns in Yourself:** Self-awareness is closely tied to emotional intelligence. Start paying attention to your emotional patterns. Are there certain situations that consistently cause you stress, frustration, or anxiety? Understanding these patterns allows you to prepare for them and respond more thoughtfully when they occur. For example, if you know that difficult conversations with parents or staff tend to trigger certain emotions, you can take time beforehand to prepare yourself emotionally and approach the conversation with more calm and clarity.

- **Communicate With Emotional Clarity:** Effective communication is not just about *what* you say, but *how* you say it. As a leader, it's important to be aware of the emotional impact your words and tone can have on others. When discussing sensitive topics or delivering feedback, aim to express your thoughts clearly while also acknowledging the emotions involved. For example, instead of simply pointing out a problem, acknowledge the effort and challenges involved: "I understand this situation has been tough, and I appreciate all the hard work you've put in. Let's discuss how we can work together to find a solution." This approach balances honesty with empathy, helping you maintain trust and collaboration.

- **Develop Emotional Resilience:** Emotional resilience is the ability to bounce back from setbacks and maintain emotional stability during stressful times. One way to build resilience is by reframing negative situations and focusing on what you can learn from them. For example, if a major initiative doesn't go as planned, instead of dwelling on the failure, ask yourself these questions: What can I learn from this experience? How can I improve next time? This shift in mindset helps you stay positive and forward-thinking, which in turn influences the morale and resilience of those you lead.

Emotional intelligence, at its core, is the ability to recognize, understand, and manage not only our own emotions but also those of others.

CULTIVATE EMPATHY FOR YOURSELF AND OTHERS

Cultivating empathy—both for yourself and for others—is a vital part of effective leadership. As education leaders, we're often focused on caring for our school communities, but it's equally important to practice self-compassion. When we can extend empathy inward, we build resilience and create a more sustainable approach to leading. Simultaneously, showing empathy toward others fosters trust, strengthens relationships, and creates a school culture where everyone feels valued and understood. Here are some suggestions to support your development of empathy for yourself and others:

- **Practice Self-Compassion:** Leadership can be a demanding and often isolating role. It's easy to be hard on yourself when things don't go as planned or when you feel overwhelmed by the responsibilities you carry. One of the most important forms of empathy is self-compassion—treating yourself with the same kindness you'd offer a friend or colleague. When you experience setbacks, instead of being self-critical, remind yourself: I'm doing my best in a challenging situation. Take time to recognize your efforts and allow yourself the space to make mistakes and grow. This mindset not only fosters emotional resilience but also models healthy self-care for your team.

- **Listen Without Judgment:** One of the most powerful ways to show empathy to others is by truly listening—without judgment, interruption, or the need to immediately offer solutions. When someone comes to you with a concern, resist the urge to problem-solve right away. Instead, give them your full attention, acknowledge their feelings, and allow them to express themselves fully. This practice validates their emotions and shows that you respect their perspective. Sometimes, simply feeling heard can help a person begin to find their own solutions.

- **Acknowledge and Validate Emotions:** As a leader, you may feel pressure to remain objective or even stoic in the face of challenges. However, empathy requires recognizing that emotions are a natural part of the human experience—both for yourself and for others. When a colleague, teacher, or student expresses frustration, anxiety, or disappointment, take a moment to acknowledge those emotions. You can say something like, "I understand why you might feel this way," or, "It sounds like you're going through a difficult time." Validating emotions doesn't mean you have to agree with everything being said, but it helps the other person feel seen and respected.

- **Practice Perspective-Taking (Putting Yourself in Others' Shoes):** Empathy involves stepping outside of our own perspective to understand what others might be feeling or experiencing. When you're faced with conflict or a difficult decision, try to see the situation through the eyes of those involved. Ask yourself: How might they be feeling? What pressures or challenges are they dealing with? This practice can help you respond with greater sensitivity, particularly when navigating complex dynamics like staff disagreements or parent concerns. By taking time to consider other viewpoints, you're more likely to find solutions that address the needs of everyone involved.

- **Create Space for Emotional Conversations:** In the fast pace of school leadership, it's easy to focus solely on tasks and outcomes. However, taking time to create space for emotional conversations can deepen empathy and connection within your school community. Encourage regular check-ins with your staff, where you can discuss not just work-related matters but also how people are feeling. Ask questions like, "How are you really doing?" or, "What's been weighing on your mind lately?" By fostering these conversations, you signal that emotions are an important and valued part of the school environment, and you help build a culture of support and understanding.

- **Extend Grace to Yourself and Others:** As leaders, we often hold ourselves and others to high standards, yet asserting high expectations on others may inadvertently cause a sense of pressure. Cultivating empathy means recognizing that we are all human—we all have limits, make mistakes, and face personal challenges. Extend grace to yourself by acknowledging when you need a break or when things didn't go as planned and offer that same grace to others. This might mean being more flexible with deadlines, offering support to a staff member going through a tough time, or recognizing that a mistake is part of the learning process. When we give ourselves and others room to grow, we foster a more compassionate and understanding environment.

- **Show Appreciation and Gratitude:** A simple yet powerful way to express empathy is through appreciation. Recognizing the efforts, challenges, and emotional investment of those around you helps build connection and reinforces a sense of belonging. Regularly take time to express gratitude to your staff, students, and colleagues, whether through verbal acknowledgment, written notes, or public recognition. Let them know that you see their hard work and understand the emotional energy they bring to their roles. This small act of empathy can go a long way in building trust and morale within your school community.

STRENGTHEN YOUR SUPPORT NETWORKS

In Chapter 9, you examined the habit "Don't Travel Alone." The habit of developing and engaging with a support network is strongly connected to your personal resilience and therefore your ability to navigate times of change as a leader. Consider these avenues for strengthening your network with a lens toward how your trusted colleagues, friends, and mentors will nurture and empower your change leadership skills. Strengthening support networks is essential for education leaders, as the demands of leadership can be both professionally and personally challenging. Having a solid support system not only helps you navigate difficult situations but also fosters collaboration, emotional well-being, and shared growth. As leaders, we sometimes forget that we, too, need help and guidance, and building a strong network ensures that you're never facing challenges alone. Here are some suggestions to help you strengthen your support networks:

- **Foster Meaningful Relationships With Your Leadership Team:** Your leadership team is one of your closest support networks within the school. Strengthening these relationships can create a more cohesive and effective team. Make time to engage with your assistant principals, department heads, or other key staff members on a personal level. Regularly check in with them, not just about work tasks, but also about how they're doing. Ask questions like, "What challenges are you facing, and how can I support you?" By fostering open communication, you build trust and deepen the sense of collaboration. When you create an environment where your team feels supported, they'll also be more likely to support you when needed.

- **Seek Out Mentorship:** No matter where we are in our careers, there's always room to learn from others who have walked the path before us. Mentorship can be a valuable resource, whether you're a new leader or a seasoned professional. Find mentors who have experience in areas where you want to grow—whether that's leadership, conflict resolution, or managing change. Reach out to experienced leaders within your district or explore leadership networks that connect you with potential mentors. Mentors provide not only guidance but also encouragement, helping you navigate complex situations with confidence and clarity.

- **Nurture Relationships With Teachers and Staff:** While your leadership team plays a central role in your support network, don't overlook the importance of nurturing strong relationships with teachers and staff. These relationships are foundational to your school's culture and can be a source of both support and insight. Create regular opportunities to engage with teachers beyond formal meetings—whether it's through informal check-ins, staff appreciation events, or even collaborative problem-solving sessions. When your staff feels valued and supported, they're more likely to offer that same support in return, helping you navigate both day-to-day and larger challenges.

- **Build a Strong Relationship With the School Board and District Leaders:** Your school board and district leaders are key players in your broader support network. Strengthening these relationships helps you gain their trust and ensures you have allies when advocating for resources or navigating systemic challenges. Take time to keep district leaders informed about the successes and challenges in your school, and don't hesitate to ask for guidance or resources when necessary. By building a foundation of trust and communication, you'll be better positioned to work collaboratively when complex issues arise.

As you lead significant change, remember that resilience is a journey, not a destination. Each challenge you face provides an opportunity to build this skill, deepening your capacity to lead with confidence and compassion. Embrace the process, knowing that through your growth, you empower others to navigate change with courage and optimism.

Resilience is a journey, not a destination. . . . Embrace the process, knowing that through your growth, you empower others to navigate change with courage and optimism.

Pause and Reflect

As you examine the various practices and mindsets for cultivating your resilience and as you strive to be utmost effective at leading during times of change, what connections did you notice from these ideas to the other habits within the book? How might you leverage one particular habit to maximize your development of resilience?

_____

_____

_____

_____

_____

The Big Ideas

In this chapter, you examined the ways in which resilient leaders are better equipped to guide themselves and their communities through change with confidence. The chapter examined the connection between purpose, values, resilience, and success in navigating change. You explored the unique mindsets of resilience that contribute to effective change leadership. Additionally, you focused on developing skills to foster self-awareness, build emotional intelligence, and develop your empathy IQ when leading others. The strategies and practices within this habit highlighted pivotal opportunities for self-development, empowering you to become a leader who actively nurtures these traits to not only enhance their own well-being but also positively influence their teams and schools.

Let's Reflect

1. What opportunities might you notice in this chapter to employ other habits within the book in support of developing your resilience as a leader of change?

   _____

   _____

   _____

2. How has your understanding of what it means to be a resilient leader evolved as you have read the various chapters of the book?

   _____

   _____

   _____

3. What new ideas from this chapter on leading change as a resilient leader will you prioritize as an area of personal growth in the immediate future?

   _____

   _____

   _____

What's Next?

As you arrive at the end of the chapters on each habit of a resilient leader, let this not be the last time you visit them. Whether you read the chapters sequentially or in an order that is best aligned with your personal growth goals, notice that each habit merits far deeper, ongoing exploration as you journey through your career in education leadership. Take advantage of the opportunity to determine a personal accountability goal for both immediate next steps to apply your learning about the habits and long-range goals for personal and professional growth. As you strive toward that goal, recall the value of your ultimate pursuit: investing in your personal well-being as a leader so that you may be of utmost service to those in your community—your staff, your students, their families, and your broader community. Happy leading!

Epilogue

A s individuals with experience in the field of education leadership, we were motivated to write this book because of the significant transformations occurring in the educational landscape for leaders, educators, students, and families. Witnessing the challenges and pressures brought about by these changes led us to feel a sense of urgency. As we observed many educators departing the profession, we engaged in discussions about the principal and leadership shortages as well as the teaching shortage and its impact on schools. The swift changes in education meant that some schools we were working with had lost a substantial portion of their leadership and teaching staff. We provided support to both new and seasoned leaders and teachers striving to create school and classroom climates conducive to academic learning, noting the absence of essential habits for fostering such environments in education leadership programs. Additionally, leaders and educators commencing their careers amidst the COVID-19 pandemic seemed to lack crucial in-person training experiences. Recognizing the need for practical and sustainable habits to promote successful school and classroom cultures, we identified resilient habits crucial for education leaders to navigate anxiety, doubt, and continuous change. Our goal is to counter the feelings of hopelessness and overwhelm that many education leaders experience and inspire confidence during ambiguous times. Our book emphasizes the importance of prioritizing standard-based instruction and student assessment while developing the identified habits. While all ten habits are crucial, we encourage readers to focus on one or two initially and utilize the interactive reflection activities within the book to engage more deeply with the content and plan intentionally to apply their learning. These habits act as drivers for ongoing growth as leaders and should be consistently incorporated into daily routines to continually enhance one's leadership skills.

Our goal is to counter the feelings of hopelessness and overwhelm that many education leaders experience and inspire confidence during ambiguous times.

SPREADING RESILIENT HABITS

In today's educational environment, the role of dedicated and knowledgeable education leaders and teachers remains indispensable despite the use of technology to support academic growth. As school culture and leadership becomes more challenging, it is crucial for both leaders and educators to develop resilient habits to promote the academic and socio-emotional development of all learners. Although embarking on the journey of adopting resilient habits can be an individual effort, the power of collective leadership and teacher efficacy is not to be underestimated. Working with colleagues to practice these habits can amplify their impact and make the process more enjoyable. Together, education leaders can enhance their resilience and regain control amid the challenges they encounter. The habits outlined in this book, when embraced collectively, create a positive ripple effect that can permeate schools and entire districts. Consistent practice of these habits, either individually or in collaboration with colleagues, transforms them into effective and efficient patterns in both personal and professional life. Consider inviting colleagues to focus on one resilient habit each month and set goals for improvement accordingly. Grant yourself the liberty to revisit chapters, reflect on your progress, and refine the habits to address evolving needs in your personal and professional contexts.

Together, education leaders can enhance their resilience and regain control amid the challenges they encounter.

References

American Psychological Association. (n.d.). *Resilience.* In APA dictionary of psychology. Retrieved December 18, 2024, from https://www.apa.org/topics/resilience

Banaji, M., & Greenwald, A. (2016). *Blindspot: Hidden biases of good people.* Bantam.

Bennis, W., & Nanus, B. (1985). *Leaders: The strategies for taking charge.* Harper & Row.

Broadwell, M. (1969, February 20). *Teaching for learning XVI.* The Gospel. Retrieved October 16, 2024, from wordsfitly spoken.com

Chapman, G. D. (2010). *The five love languages.* Walker Large Print.

Cherry, K. (2023, December 7). *Why you may not know how to connect with people.* Verywell Mind. https://www.verywellmind.com/i-cant-connect-with-people-why-you-might-feel-this-way-5219583

Clear, J. (2018). *Atomic habits: An easy & proven way to build good habits & break bad ones.* Penguin.

Cloud, H. (2013). *Boundaries for leaders: Results, relationships, and being ridiculously in charge.* Harper Business.

Danielson, C., Furman, J., & Kappes, L. (2024). *Enhancing professional practice* (3rd ed.). ASCD.

Diamond, J., Zigarmi, L., & Mones, L. (2024, June 13). *5 traps to avoid as you gain power as a leader.* Harvard Business Review.

Fernandez, K., Clerkin, C., & Ruderman, M. (2020). *Building leadership resilience with the CORE framework.* Center for Creative Leadership.

Fullan, M., & Quinn, J. (2015). *Coherence: The right drivers in action for schools, districts, and systems.* Corwin.

Goddard, R., Hoy, W., & Hoy, A. (2004). Collective efficacy beliefs: Theoretical developments, empirical evidence, and future directions. *Educational Researcher, 33*(3), 3–13.

Hattie, J. (2015). High-impact leadership. *Educational Leadership, 72*(5), 36–40.

Hattie, J. (2023, April 18). *How great teachers think.* Edutopia. https://www.edutopia.org/article/great-teachers-engage-evaluative-thinking/

Hattie, J., Fisher, D., Frey, N., & Almarode, J. (2024). *The illustrated guide to visible learning.* Illustrations by T. Hansen. Corwin.

Health Coach Institute. (2023, June 16). *7 types of self-care & why you need them.* Holistic Health and Wellness Training. Health Coach Institute. https://www.healthcoachinstitute.com/articles/7-types-of-self-care/

Hopkin, M. R. (2016, May 2). *Why great leaders are learners.* https://leadonpurposeblog.com/2016/05/02/why-great-leaders-are-learners/

Hoy, W., Sweetland, S., & Smith, P. (2002). Toward an organizational model of achievement in high schools: The significance of collective efficacy. *Education Administration Quarterly, 38*(1), 77–93.

Jussim, L., & Harber, K. D. (2005). Teacher expectations and self-fulfilling prophecies: Knowns and unknowns resolved and unresolved controversies. *Perspectives on Psychological Science, 1*(3), 263–287.

Kim, E. S., Strecher, V. J., & Ryff, C. D. (2014). Purpose in life and use of preventive health care services. *Proceedings of the National Academy of Sciences, 111*(46), 16331–16336.

Lee, T., & Dance, B. (2022, August 18). *The connection between purpose and resiliency.* Mercer.

Lofgren, J. (2021, May 17). *The role that boundaries play in leadership growth.* Retrieved November 10, 2023, from Forbes.com

Lu, S., Elliott, S., & Perlman, C. (2019). Perceived facilitators and barriers to evaluative thinking in a small development NGO. *Canadian Journal of Program Evaluation, 34*(1).

Martin, S. (2018, April 24). *What are boundaries and why do I need them?* Retrieved November 8, 2023, from www.livewellwithsharonmartin.com/what-are-boundaries/

Medor, D. (2019, February 20). *How teachers can build a trusting relationship with their principal.* Retrieved November 3, 2023, from https://www.thoughtco.com/build-a-trusting-relationship-with-their-principal-3194349

NASSP. (2022). *Understanding and addressing principal turnover.* https://www.nassp.org/publication/principal-leadership/

National Association of Secondary School Principals. (n.d.). *Principal Leadership.* Retrieved January 11, 2025, from https://www.nassp.org/publication/principal-leadership/

National Center for Health Statistics. (2021). *NHANES 2021 - NHANES questionnaires, datasets, and related documentation.* https://wwwn.cdc.gov/nchs/nhanes/continuousnhanes/default.aspx?Cycle=2021-2023

Nauck, F., Pancaldi, L., Poppensieker, T., & White, O. (2021). *The resilience imperative: Succeeding uncertain times.* McKinsey & Company.

Patel, K. J. (2020). *Burning bright: Rituals, reiki, and self-care to heal burnout, anxiety, and stress.* Random House.

Patel, L. (2024, February 20). The power of effective communication in leadership. *Forbes.* https://www.forbes.com/sites/forbesbusinessdevelopmentcouncil/2023/09/05/the-power-of-effective-communication-in-leadership/

Peaceful Schools. (2013). *Peaceful schools - We help students use their power to be peaceful.* https://peacefulschools.com/

Prendergast, L., & Lee, P. (2024). *Habits of resilient educators: Strategies for thriving during times of anxiety, doubt, and constant change.* Corwin.

Rickards, F., Hattie, J., & Reid, C. (2020). *The turning point for the teaching profession growing expertise and evaluative thinking.* Routledge.

Sahlin, S. (2022). Teachers making sense of principals' leadership in collaboration within and beyond school. *Scandinavian Journal of Educational Research, 67*(5), 754–774. https://doi.org/10.1080/00313831.2022.2043429

Scott, K. (2019). *Radical candor: Fully revised & updated edition: Be a kick-ass boss without losing your humanity.* St. Martin's Press.

Seif, E. (2024). *Integrating Professional Learning Communities (PLCs) and the Lifelong Learning Education (LLE) Framework.* Solution Tree Blog. https://www.solutiontree.com/blog/integrating-professional-learning-communities-plcs-and-the-lifelong-learning-education-lle-framework/

Southwick, S., & Charney, D. (2018). *Resilience: The science of mastering life's greatest challenges* (2nd ed.). Cambridge University Press.

Thought Collective. (2023, March 16). *Mastering non-verbal communication: A leaders guide.* Thought Collective. https://www.jointhecollective.com/article/non-verbal-communication-in-leadership

Tuckman, B. W. (1965). Developmental sequence in small groups. *Psychological Bulletin, 63*(6), 384–399. https://doi.org/10.1037/h0022100

Waite, R. (2024). *Coaching industry report: Insights, trends, and statistics.* https://www.robinwaite.com/coaching-industry-report

Weiss, M., Razinskas, S., Backmann, J., & Hoegl, M. (2018). Authentic leadership and leaders' mental well-being: An experience sampling study. *The Leadership Quarterly, 29*(2), 309–321.

Wellman, B., & Lipton, L. (2017). *Data-driven dialogue a facilitator's guide to collaborative inquiry* (2nd ed.). MiraVia.

Wiseman, L. (2021). *Impact players: How to take the lead, play bigger, and multiply your impact.* Harper.

World Health Organization. (n.d.). Self-care for health and well-being. *World Health Organization.* Retrieved May 2024 from https://www.who.int/news-room/questions-and-answers/item/self-care-for-health-and-well-being

Index

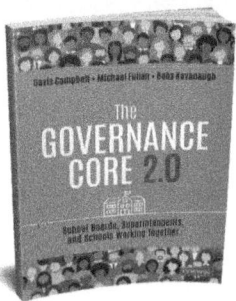

Free Professional Development

WEBINARS

Listen and interact with education experts for an hour of professional learning to gain practical tools and evidence-based strategies—and maybe win some free books!

LEADERS COACHING LEADERS PODCAST

Join Peter M. DeWitt, Michael Nelson, and their guests as they discuss evidence-based approaches for tackling pressing topics that all education leaders face.

CORWIN CONNECT

Read and engage with us on our blog about the latest in education and professional development.

SAMPLE CONTENT

Did you know you can download sample content from almost every Corwin book on our website? Go to corwin.com/resources for tools you and your staff can use right away!

SOCIAL JUSTICE RESEARCH

Takeaways for K–12 from the latest research on advancing educational equity and justice.

CORWIN

CORWIN

To help every educator
help every student

We believe that every single student
deserves a great education

We believe that knowing our impact is both
a privilege and a responsibility

We believe that a fair, stable, and thriving
society is built on education

THE PROFESSIONAL LEARNING ASSOCIATION

Learning Forward is a nonprofit, international membership association of learning educators committed to one vision in K–12 education: Equity and excellence in teaching and learning. To realize that vision, Learning Forward pursues its mission to build the capacity of leaders to establish and sustain highly effective professional learning. Information about membership, services, and products is available from www.learningforward.org.